KINGOLOGY
The Return of The King

R.C. BLAKES, JR.

KINGOLOGY
The Return of the Kings

Copyright 2020 by R.C. Blakes, Jr.

Unless otherwise noted, scripture quotations
are taken from the Holy Bible, King James version.

All rights reserved. No part of this publication may be reproduced, stored in a retrieval system, or transmitted in any form by means electronic, mechanical, photocopying, recording or otherwise, except for the inclusion of brief quotations in a review, without prior permission in writing from the publisher.

ISBN: 978-1-7335050-5-5 (paperback)

PUBLISHED BY

UP
UNTAPPED POTENTIAL
PUBLISHING

P.O. Box 84355
Pearland, Tx 77584

Digital book(s) (epub and mobi) produced by Booknook.biz.

Dedication

Firstly, this book is dedicated to the men in my life. Every man needs a team of men around him to keep him steady and inspired. The main man in my life who formed and shaped me was my father, Bishop Robert Blakes, Sr. He was the first king I witnessed. My concept of manhood came from the example he modeled. He established a standard that continues to set the bar. As a young boy, when I looked at my dad, I saw a king. Rest in peace.

Secondly, I want to dedicate this work to my brother, Bishop Samuel Blakes. You are a strong and powerful man, like our father. You are a king in the eyes of the world and your family. Thank you for being my best friend and confidant.

The third king I want to dedicate this book to is my son, Robert Blakes III. Though you are very different and unique within yourself, you are frighteningly similar to the men of our family. You are a Blakes man. You possess your grandfather's humility and benevolence. You have attained your Uncle Sam's friendly and magnetizing personality and you've managed to manifest your father's love for solitude and thought. You are one of the most authentic men I know. Greatness is your portion. Remember this: Being great is not measured in accolades, material gain, money or power; greatness is measured in authenticity. Be true to your own heart. Follow the path that gives you a sense of fulfillment and gives the heart of God pleasure. Be great.

This book is also dedicated to my Three Kings (grandsons), Alvex, Austin and Amir. You guys are amazing. The future of our family is in good hands. Thank you for adding so much love and purpose to this season of your grandfather's life. Always take care of your responsibilities. Take care of each other. Be honest and fight for the people you love. You are kings!

Finally, this book is also dedicated to the men of New Home Ministries. I am honored to be your pastor. I thank God for giving me the privilege of leading an army of kings. Thank you for trusting me.

R.C. Blakes, Jr.

Contents

Foreword by Robert Charles Blakes III   vii
Introduction   ix

Chapter 1
THE TRUE MEASURE OF A KING
What Actually Makes a Man?
1

Chapter 2
KING CONSCIOUSNESS
Manhood Is Not Chronological; It's Psychological
19

Chapter 3
THINGS THAT RUIN KINGS
Things That Will Destroy a Man's Greatness
33

Chapter 4
UNDERSTANDING THE TENSION BETWEEN
KINGS AND QUEENS
The Spiritual and Social Complexities between
Men and Women
51

Chapter 5
KINGS ARE INTENTIONAL ABOUT RELATIONSHIPS
Kings Are Not Random or Irresponsible in Relationships
67

Chapter 6
THE HARMONY OF KINGS AND QUEENS
How Kings and Queens Find Each Other and
Function in Sync
93

Chapter 7
KINGS AND COINS
A King's Respect for Money
107

Chapter 8
KINGS REGULATE THEIR EMOTIONS
Kings Maintain Control of Their Internal Stability
121

Conclusion
135

Foreword
By Robert Charles Blakes III

The definition of a king has evolved with the times. As monarchies are no longer as prominent today, we must ask ourselves, what makes someone a king in today's world? I would argue that a king in this era would be a man who is in tune with his spiritual, emotional, financial, and mental responsibilities. A king is someone who follows God's guidelines for being a man.

My father, R.C. Blakes Jr. has been the best example of a man that I could have asked for in a father. Throughout my life, he has exemplified what it means to truly be a king in this world. From handling his finances and overcoming setbacks, to being a God-fearing and respectful father and husband, he really does practice what he preaches. He uses God's word and his own life experiences to not only be the best example of a king he can be, but also to teach and share his knowledge with others.

In this book, he will tackle the obstacles faced by true kings and men of God in today's society. He has an understanding of what a king looks like, and a true desire to be one in every area of his life. In this book, R.C. Blakes Jr. will share some of that understanding and help other men transform their lives into that of king-conscious men.

Robert Blakes III (AKA Tre Blakes)
Sophomore at the University of Arizona

Introduction

In recent generations it appears that there has been a decline in the quality of manhood. When we look at the great numbers of fatherless children, and at women who are carrying the entire family, this doesn't reflect the values of classical (biblical) manhood. The irresponsibility and narcissistic mind-set of this generation of men looks nothing like the strength and sacrifice of men from a couple of generations ago. Men who are ordained to reign as kings have degenerated into something far less than the regal rulers God ordained. It makes me want to grab these brothers and shake them and scream, "Wake up! You are a king!"

I love the game of chess, though I rarely get to play, and am probably too distracted to be very good anymore. When I see a chessboard, I see a reflection of life and the family. The board represents a kingdom. The various pieces represent the players in that kingdom, from king and queen all the way down the food chain to the pawns.

The world is filled with pawns. A pawn is the sacrificial piece of the game. It is considered by most people to be the least significant piece in most game scenarios. On a chessboard there are more pawns than any other piece: eight pawns, compared to a pair of knights, a pair of rooks and a pair of bishops. The interesting fact is that there is only one king and one queen; pawns are in abundance.

In the game, the loss of a pawn is largely inconsequential and forgettable. When a pawn is sacrificed, nobody laments the loss as some irreversible damage done to the outcome of the game in general. When I think of a pawn, I imagine that it can be psychologically compared to many of the men in modern society. Most men are not truly making any significant impact on the world. Most men are group thinkers. Most men are pawns, easily forgotten, and make no real impact on the overall grand scheme of life. Think about how many guys you know whose lives are presently counting for nothing but sex, money and clothes. If they were to die today, there wouldn't be much to remember them for.

Kings Do Not Live Forgettable Lives.

Another characterization of modern society's representation of manhood would be a comparison to the court jester. The jester was the clown of the kingdom. He existed to amuse others at the expense of his own dignity. When we take an honest look at society, today's men are quite often a joke. We become a joke to our families and even to society when we lack the king consciousness that extracts the king from within.

Our values and standards are so out of sync with the psychology of a real man that we are not to be taken seriously. Our women don't respect us, our children don't acknowledge us, and society often disregards us. In some cases, the dis by society is unwarranted, but in too many cases it is actually earned.

With all of this being stated, I am aware that there are particular and intentional systematic structures designed to emasculate or debilitate the man, and even to take certain segments of men out of the family dynamic. These things are indisputable.

However, it's another matter altogether when we as men live irresponsibly; this only exacerbates the problem. For instance, it's not institutional racism that causes a man to dishonor the mother of his children. It's not feminism that makes a man show up for a job late three days a week until he gets fired and possibly replaced by a woman. These are jester-like characteristics that the man has to own. Manhood is about taking responsibility.

A Jester Is a Man Just Like the King, but the Kingdom Does Not Struggle at the Absence of a Jester.

Jesters are easily replaced. Any fool can be the joke. The kingdom is looking for the strength of a king, the wisdom of a patriarch and the security of a strong man. Kingdoms suffer at the absence of kings. While the pawn is forgotten, and jesters are easily replaced, kings are indispensable. The aim of this book is to encourage you to be an indispensable man.

The World Is Awaiting the Return of the King.

In my book, *Queenology*, the sister book to *Kingology*, written to the empowerment of women, I open the book with a fictional tale about a king by the name of King Paternum and his queen, Queen Materno. In the story, the king was away from the kingdom and we learn that, during that time, the queen died. After the queen's death some evil subjects took advantage of the king's three young daughters. They indoctrinated the princesses to believe that they were slaves and servants. They robbed them of their queen consciousness. When the king unexpectedly returned to discover the psychological abuse that had been exacted on his daughters, he beheaded all of those responsible.

One part of the story that is not revealed in that book is that the queen didn't just die while the king was absent; she was poisoned. She was assassinated by the same people who abused his daughters. They wanted to usurp the power of the kingdom in the king's absence.

When the Kings Are Absent, the Kingdom (Family) Is Vulnerable.

The enemies of the kingdom took advantage of the king's absence and destroyed his family. In the game of chess, the opponent does not win until the king is overturned.

In the story, as the king settled into his new reality, he began to look over his life as a man and to unpack the pros and cons of his reign as a king, husband and father. Where did he succeed? Where did he fail? What would he have done differently if he could have lived his life over again? What lessons did he want to leave for future kings?

The king never had any sons, but he did eventually have sons-in-law and grandsons. In his later years, he took the time to revisit some of the mistakes he had made as a man and a king. One of the things he dedicated his life to was to train the young men in his kingdom, based on his lifetime of experience. He called this course of study "Kingology" (The study of kings). The king was no fool; if his daughters were to have suitable mates, the kingdom required a generation of king-conscious men.

It Takes a King to Train a King.

CHAPTER 1

THE TRUE MEASURE OF A KING
What Actually Makes a Man?

You will notice throughout this document that I will use the terms "man" and "king" interchangeably. For some, this might be a bit unsettling, seeing that society has done everything possible to rob the man of his king consciousness. Society has robbed the man of the very concept of man being anything more than financial and sexual. Pure manhood is so much more.

What is a man? Depending on what sector of society might be asked this question, we will return with a myriad of answers. Were we to ask a young adolescent male, he would probably say, "A man is a male of twenty-one years of age or more." If we were to settle on the most perverted chauvinistic concept of manhood, we might return with the idea that a man is one who manipulates multiple relationships with females, while avoiding commitment to any. In other words, a man is a "player." Others might associate a man with money and fashion. A man is always fashion-forward and physically attractive to women. If we took this question to academia, a man might be one who strives for and achieves power and success in his chosen discipline of study and expertise. If we brought the question to religious circles, he might be one who subjugates his wife based on biblical misconceptions of submission. If we took the question to the most wealthy people of the world, a man might be one who can increase the bottom line substantially, from generation to generation. We would get a lot of different answers.

When manhood is not clearly defined, would-be men tend to vacillate between the many ideas of manhood, never anchoring themselves in a true and consistent or reliable concept.

The famous and brilliant man himself, Myles Monroe, once said, "If you want the true purpose or definition of a thing you must go back to the manufacturer and creator of the thing." God is the maker of man; therefore, God has the true answer regarding the absolute definition of a man. So again, I ask the question: "What is man?"

WHAT IS MAN?

The Bible asks the question in Psalms 8:4–6: *What is man, that thou art mindful of him? and the son of man, that thou visitest him? For thou hast made him a little lower than the angels, and hast crowned him with glory and honor. Thou madest him to have dominion over the works of thy hands; thou hast put all things under his feet.*

This is a text that specifically describes God's evaluation of who and what a man is. I love this text for the revelation it provides every young and older male, relative to the Creator's view of what you are, what you're worth and who you are. The Bible says, "God has crowned man with glory and honor." Crowning is a sacred declaration reserved for establishing royalty.

God himself established and positioned man in a place of dignity, authority and royalty in the universe. When God made Adam (man), God crowned him (king).

When I was a child, I played the game checkers a lot. I guess you can tell that we played board games when I was growing up. However, in the game, if one got his checker to the farthermost row into his opponent's territory, he could call for his opponent to "king me." This meant that that particular piece had almost godlike ability, within the game, to make moves that were unthinkable. The king could do horrendous damage to the enemy's agenda, all because it had been crowned. When God crowned man, he gave him the power and authority of a king.

MAN IS THE DESIGNATED KING OVER GOD'S CREATION

Genesis 1:26 says: *And God said, Let us make man in our image, after our likeness: and let them have dominion over the fish of the sea, and over the fowl of the air, and over the cattle, and over all the earth, and over every creeping thing that creepeth upon the earth.*

As God has dominion over everything, he ordained it so, that man should dominate the world and all that is in it. Man is king. God is King of kings. Man is the delegated ruler of the earth.

> A Man Is Designed to Be the Visible Expression of God on the Earth. Man Is to Be the Container of God's Glory and the Custodian of God's Power to Dominate the Earth.

I already understand that most men have not been introduced to God's true view of who they are, so the previous statement may not be digested so quickly. Just as most women do not see themselves as queens in God's great plan, most men have a severely diminished perspective of who they are.

The driving force behind this fractured perspective of manhood is due to searching for a definition from all but the right source.

When You Consult Your Sexuality, Social Status or Economic Position to Define Your Manhood, You Will Always Come Up Short.

A man must return to the foundation of his being to discover and to define himself. A man must reconcile his relationship with his creator if he is to have any hope of ever being who he really is. A man only rises to the full capacity of his potential to the extent that he has a real relationship and fellowship with God.

Kings Are Crowned, and Only God Can Ordain a King.

True kings are aware that they are only in authority to the extent that they are under authority. As long as Adam was in alignment with God, his kingdom was fine. The moment Adam got out of sync with God, it all fell apart. His being in authority was predicated upon his being under authority.

The greatest challenge for men today is that there is a lack of respect for the spiritual. A man will never be king without the endorsement and hand of God. Don't be mistaken; I am not talking religion here. This is greater than religion. This transcends institutions. This overshadows preachers and organizations. This gets to the heart of a man's genuine and personal connection to his creator.

When a Man Walks Away from God, He Abandons His Throne, Loses His Crown and Is Stripped of His Kingdom.

When a man does not have the breath of the Spirit of God, he ultimately lacks the power to master his kingdom or to manifest his total manhood. A man apart from God functions like a base being; he is sexual, cerebral and physical but he lacks the innate spirit of dominion. Dominion is the sole product of the spiritual component of the man.

A Man Walks in Dominion to the Extent That He Walks with God.

When we look at the origin of the man (Adam) in Genesis 2:7, the Bible says: *And the Lord God formed man of the dust of the ground and breathed into his nostrils the breath of life; and man became a living soul.*

The message of this passage is that Adam was complete in three parts: he was physical, spiritual and intellectual. Notice how God formed Adam from dust, which speaks of him being physical. When God breathed into Adam, he became a living soul, which speaks of him possessing the capacity to think; he was soulish. The spirit that God breathed into Adam was God's spirit, which ignited Adam's spiritual faculties; he was conscious of God. Adam was body, soul and spirit.

A Man Who Is Only Physical and Out of Balance Spiritually Is Incomplete in His Development.

Let's get into some definitions of manhood. Most men have never thought this idea through and have settled for the crude and unsophisticated definition used by generations of unenlightened males. That definition sounds a lot like this: *A man is an adult person who is male, as opposed to female.* This definition is not incorrect; it is simply incomplete.

If this definition is all there is to manhood, it means that every male who procreates (makes children) is automatically considered a man. The reality may be that he doesn't provide for those children or have any respect for their mother, but he is still to be considered a man. I wouldn't agree with that. It would also indicate that every able-bodied male who refuses to get a job and settles for living off a gullible woman or off government assistance is a man. I can't go with that either. According to the previous definition, a male who uses his strength to abuse women and children is legitimately a man. This certainly cannot be so!

True Manhood Has Little to Do with Age and More to Do with Character and Responsibility.

The truest measure of manhood is about character and responsibility, not age and sex! There's a text in the Bible that demonstrates that manhood supersedes age.

We see a powerful revelation about true manhood from David's life and in his famous battle with Goliath. Goliath was the Philistine warrior or giant who defied Israel. Goliath called for a man to fight him and no man of age responded.

Let's look at the story in 1 Samuel 17:4–10: *And there went out a champion out of the camp of the Philistines, named Goliath, of Gath, whose height was six cubits and a span. (verse 5) And he had an helmet of brass upon his head, and he was armed with a coat of mail; and the weight of the coat was five thousand shekels of brass. (verse 6) And he had greaves of brass upon his legs, and a target of brass between his shoulders. (verse 7) And the staff of his spear was like a weaver's beam; and his spear's head weighed six hundred shekels of iron: and one bearing a shield went before him. (verse 8) And he stood and cried unto the armies of Israel, and said unto* them, *Why are ye come out to set your battle in array? am not I a Philistine, and ye servants to Saul? choose you a man for you, and let him come down to me. (verse 9) If he be able to fight with me, and to kill me, then will we be your servants: but if I prevail against him, and kill him, then shall ye be our servants, and serve us. (verse 10) And the Philistine said, I defy the armies of Israel this day; give me a man, that we may fight together.*

We see in these verses that Goliath called for a man and none of the older men were willing to respond. Let's see who responded to the challenge in the following verses.

The story continues in 1 Samuel 17:24–29: *And all the men of Israel, when they saw the man, fled from him, and were sore afraid. (verse 25) And the men of Israel said, Have ye seen this man that is come up? surely to defy Israel is he come up: and it shall be, that the man who killeth him, the king will enrich him with great riches, and will give him his daughter, and make his father's house free in Israel. (verse 26) And David spake to the men that stood by him, saying, What shall be done to the man that killeth this Philistine, and taketh away the reproach from Israel? for who is this uncircumcised Philistine, that he should defy the armies of the living God? (verse 27) And the people answered him after this manner, saying, So shall it be done to the man that killeth him. (verse 28) And Eliab his eldest brother heard when he spake unto the men; and Eliab's anger was kindled against David, and he said, Why camest thou down hither? and with whom hast thou left those few sheep in the wilderness? I know thy pride, and the naughtiness of thine heart; for thou art come down that thou mightest see the battle. (verse 29) And David said, what have I now done? Is there not a cause?*

The end of the story is that David, a mere kid, stepped up to the challenge and defeated Goliath when males of full age were afraid to do so. David was a kid, but he responded when others were afraid.

A Man Is Not Determined by Years; a Man Is Determined by Character.

Character is the person's willingness and strength to do what is godly, courageous and responsible. A man is best discerned when times are challenging.

Manhood Is About Response Ability (Responsibility).

A male is a man when he is equipped to respond to God, family, society and crisis in a functional, supportive, protective and effective manner, and not until then.

David had the body of a boy but the spirit of a king (man). Kings respond where average people shrink. The difference between men and boys is the ability and willingness to respond, even if you're afraid.

AREAS WHERE KINGS RESPOND

1. Kings (Men) Respond by Parenting Their Children.
2. Kings (Men) Respond by Leading Their Families Spiritually.
3. Kings (Men) Respond by Financially Providing for Their Own.

The myth is that one may claim manhood automatically after twenty-one years of living. Quite frankly, I know many grey-haired boys. In fact, I know some boys who are grandfathers. You are not a man until you have the willingness and the capacity to respond to life. Men do not allow their women to shoulder the weight. Men respond.

True Manhood Must Be Proven and Verified.

There's an interesting conversation that King David had, much later in his life, with his son, Solomon, about manhood. This happened just before David died. The fact that David is transitioning in this text puts even greater weight on his words. A man's dying words are his most significant.

Take note of David's words to Solomon in 1 Kings 2:1–2: *Now the days of David drew nigh that he should die; and he charged Solomon his son, saying, I go the way of all the earth: be thou strong therefore, and shew thyself a man.*

David instructs Solomon to be certain to demonstrate his manhood. He says, "Show yourself a man." In other words, David is saying to his young son, "Don't assume that people will respect you as a man; demonstrate your manhood." *The interesting fact is that Solomon was just twelve years old at the time.* Manhood is not in the years; it is in the person's character.

KINGS ARE NOT BORN; THEY ARE FORMED

There's a spiritual, cerebral and natural process involved in the formation of men. Most males never embrace the process and pressure of formation.

The World Teaches Us That We Are an Island and Everything We Need Is Within Us, Apart from Anyone or Anything Else. Nothing Does Greater Damage to the Would-Be Man.

In Genesis, Adam was formed by the hand of God. Firstly, the formation of a man is always the product of something outside of the man himself. A man cannot form himself. A man is primarily formed by his creator, God. Secondly, as we will see in later chapters, a man is intended to be guided and adjusted by the wisdom of more experienced men who love and support him. This entire process calls for the man to do something that doesn't come naturally; it requires him to submit.

There Is No Such Thing as a Self-Made Man. A Self-Made Man Is at Best a Half-Made Man.

The reason for the lack of real kings today is the disconnect from the God factor. Man is the product of God.

The Bible says, in Genesis 2:7: *And the Lord God formed man of the dust of the ground.* From the very start, man was formed. He doesn't just evolve; he has to be intentionally shaped and even squeezed into form. He wasn't a tadpole that turned into a monkey that learned how to talk and think. Man was formed by God.

When we observe the process of Adam's formation, we learn great wisdom as it pertains to how men are established.

1. MEN ARE MADE UNDER PRESSURE

The first thing we may take away is that men are formed under pressure. The Bible says, in Genesis 2:7: *And the Lord God formed man of the dust of the ground.*

The term "formed" comes from the Hebrew word *yāṣar*: a verb meaning to form, to fashion, to shape, to devise. The primary meaning of the word is derived from the idea of cutting or framing. It may also be translated as "squeezed into existence."

All of the Other Aspects of God's Creation Were Spoken into Existence. Man Was Formed Under Pressure.

A part of the development of a man is always going to take place under pressure. One of the most detrimental actions the parent of a male child can take is to shelter him from all pressure. Men are developed under pressure.

The psalmist says, in Psalms 119:71: *It is good for me that I have been afflicted; that I might learn thy statutes.*

When a Man Is Robbed of His Pressure Moments, His Emotional and Spiritual Development Are Hindered.

Many Women Do Not Trust Certain Men to Lead Because They Are Too Weak, for This Very Reason.

Every man should expect and embrace the pressures of life. Pressure does for the man the same thing it does for carbon deposits; it exposes the diamond within.

Kings Are Processed Under Pressure.

2. A MAN MUST POSSESS GOD'S SPIRIT

Not only was Adam formed under pressure, but he possessed the life of God. A man is always incomplete without the life of God. The Word of God states, in Genesis 2:7: *and breathed into his nostrils the breath of life.* The breath of life was the Spirit of God possessing Adam. When a man does not have his relationship secure with God, he then lacks the emotional and spiritual depth to function as head of the family and society. He may be a great earner but fails to connect as a servant to his family. When he lacks his connection to God, something is always off. There's a deep sense of unfulfillment.

The Bible puts it best in 1 Corinthians 11:3, in the Amplified version: *...but I want you to know and realize that Christ is the Head of every man, the head of a woman is her husband, and the Head of Christ is God.*

Without the Spirit of God, the male is ill-equipped to serve as the head of anything, especially not a wife and family.

The True Power of a King Lies in His Connection to the Supreme King of Kings.

Adam had to have the life of God in his being to even qualify to rule over creation and to serve as the head of Eve.

When I think about the twenty-four years of marriage that I have been so honored and blessed to share with my wife, Lisa, at the writing of this book, it would not have been possible to lead my wife without the guidance of the Holy Spirit. I am not smart enough to know the answers or strong enough to carry the weight of responsibility it takes to lead my wife. If I did not have the Holy Spirit alive and present in my heart, I would faint.

> The Worst Thing a Man May Do Is to Attempt to Lead Without Being Led.

A man, according to God's order, is a spiritual being. Adam did not become conscious and vibrant until the Spirit of God was breathed into him. Without the spiritual deposit, you are nothing but a form.

Every man should seek God on his own terms, separate and apart from religious ritual, and should lead his family into worship. You cannot lead where you do not first go yourself.

3. A MAN HAS TO SANCTIFY HIS MIND-SET

When the Bible says, *God breathed into him and man became a living soul*, the term "soul" speaks of the man's thoughts and emotions.

> Without the Man's Soul Lining Up, He's Just a Shell. He Looks Like a Man, but He Can't Function Until His Mind-Set Is Sanctified.

The Word of God puts it in these terms, in Proverbs 23:7: *For as he thinketh in his heart so he is.*

> You Are Nothing More or Less Than What Is on Your Mind Constantly.

To be a man, in the biblical sense, you will have to have your soul sanctified. Your thought life must be adjusted and purged.

Here's a bit of my uncomfortable truth as a man: I have not always been the man that I am today. I am the evidence of grace and mercy. I am the outcome of a divine process. When I was a teenaged boy of fifteen years of age, I became a teen father, out of wedlock. Wanting to make things right, I married the mother of my young child at eighteen years of age. That marriage did not work. I was the father of a child, but I was not yet a man. I was old enough to go into the military or to drive a car, but I was not yet a man. I lacked the capacity to function as a leader for a wife and family; I was not yet a man.

I was an adulterer. I was never faithful to any woman. My perspective of manhood was skewed by the opinions of broken men who came before me. I had a limited and crude view of manhood. Needless to say, my marriage did not last.

After that marriage came to an end, I married another young lady. I was in my very early twenties. I meant well, but I was undeveloped. That marriage also came to an end because my mind-set was too deficient to shoulder the weight of such responsibility.

You Cannot Function as a Man When You Think Like a Boy.

You may locate the level of your thinking by observing your dominant behavior. If you're behaving like a boy in puberty, you know your consciousness level.

The Apostle Paul said, in 1 Corinthians 13:11: *When I was a child, I spake as a child, I understood as a child, I thought as a child: but when I became a man, I put away childish things.*

Notice, he said that when he became a man, he put childish behavior aside. After my second failed marriage

I decided that I was going to get myself together as a man and get my mind right.

> I Shifted in My Mind-Set Long Before My Consistent Behavior Mirrored It.

To make a long story short, God delivered me from all of my sexual vices and perversion. I learned, as a young Christian man, what it felt like to live a life of sexual abstinence. God synced my lifestyle with my values and my message.

I began to grow and mature in my manhood. I was a young minister and I was proud to say that my message and my life were mostly in sync. My mind shift was the key to my entire life transformation as a man.

By the time I married Lisa, my mind-set had been sanctified. I was a king who was mentally prepared for a queen. At the writing of this book, we've been married for twenty-four years and are still very happily married, without any incidents. Why? This is because my mind-set has been purified and my lifestyle has followed. Every man owes it to the woman he chooses to be his wife to be certain that his mind-set, as a man, is developed in godliness.

4. A MAN MUST HAVE AN AWARENESS OF HIS GOD PURPOSE

In Genesis 2:15, it says: *And the Lord God took the man and put him into the garden of Eden to dress it and to keep it.*

When God breathed His Spirit into Adam, it was God sanctifying Adam's mind-set. He simultaneously awakened Adam's awareness of his purpose. Adam knew his "why." God made Adam know why he existed. It will always be a difficult challenge to live a life of consistency and purpose if a man does not have a firm understanding of his "why." Do you know why you exist?

Only God Can Make a Man Aware of His Purpose Because God Is the Architect of the Man's Purpose.

A huge part of the man's formation is in doing the internal work necessary to discover what the Almighty has placed within him. Just like Adam knew that God created him to keep the garden, he will make every man aware of his "why."

The Problem with Society Today Is That Men Lack Purpose. When Men Lack Purpose, Self-Destruction Is Inevitable.

Proverbs 29:18 says: *Where there is no vision, the people perish.* In other words, when a person does not have a clearly defined God-given "why," they ultimately live chaotic and lawless lives. It is after a man discovers his purpose that he takes authority over his passions. A man has to have something that's more important than base impulses and instincts.

A Man Who Is Recklessly Sexual Has Not Yet Discovered His Purpose.

5. A MAN IS FORMED UNDER DIVINE AUTHORITY IN HIS LIFE

Again, in Genesis 2:16–17, it says: *And the Lord God commanded the man, saying, Of every tree of the garden thou mayest freely eat: (verse 17). But of the tree of the knowledge of good and evil, thou shalt not eat of it: for in the day that thou eatest thereof thou shalt surely die.*

Divine authority was introduced to Adam from the very start. Adam had to understand that he was only in authority to the extent that he was properly positioned under authority.

One of the chief struggles of men is the inability and unwillingness to submit to authority. A man cannot just do whatever he desires to do. God has established laws and principles that are to govern a man's life.

Hebrews 12:11 says, in the Amplified version: *For the time being no discipline brings joy, but seems grievous and painful; but afterwards it yields a peaceable fruit of righteousness to those who have been trained by it [a harvest of fruit which consists in righteousness—in conformity to God's will in purpose, thought, and action, resulting in right living and right standing with God].*

This is the main purpose and necessity of fathers in the lives of their sons. A father is supposed to function as the authority in his son's life as he develops. When fathers are absent from the lives of their sons, it distorts all of society. A man being under authority is fundamental to his evolution as a man.

CHAPTER 2

KING CONSCIOUSNESS
Manhood Is Not Chronological;
It's Psychological

As I walk the earth today, I live as a conscious man. I know who I am, and I know why I'm here. Nobody may mislead or deceive me; I am conscious.

What is consciousness? To be conscious is to be physically, emotionally, socially or spiritually aware and responsive to God, to one's self and to one's community. Consciousness is the capacity to understand and control what is going on within one's self, as well as what's happening around you.

> The Distinguishing Marker Between Manhood and Boyhood Is Consciousness.

A little boy has all of the physical parts of a grown man. The thing that transitions a boy into a man is consciousness. As for me, when I actually evolved into manhood, I discovered that my self-knowledge, coupled with my ability to manage myself and my environment, empowered me to behave like a king. I believe that the big difference between grown boys versus grown men is consciousness.

> Boys Are Driven, Like Slaves, by Their Feral (Uncontrollable) Passions, While Men Are in Control of Themselves and Their Environment, Like Kings.

From the time I was a young boy, I had been sexually out of control. I reacted to every sexual whim. I actually believed that my manhood was hitched to my sexual conquests. One day, after a serious encounter with God and an abrupt self-awakening, I found myself in control of everything that had previously driven me like a slave.

My God consciousness led me into self-awareness, which shifted the paradigm. I went from slave to master. All of this because of an adjustment to my consciousness.

Manhood Happens Between the Ears. A Man Thinks a Certain Way.

When we observe the biblical parable (story) of the Prodigal son, we see something. The account actually shows us the evolution of a boy into a man and it was all because of the way he thought about himself and life. Though the boy went from riches to rags and back to riches, nothing changed about the young man but his consciousness. Broken consciousness drove him away from his best life and a return to consciousness restored him.

The parable is recorded in Luke 15:11–20, where it says: *And he said, A certain man had two sons: And the younger of them said to his father, Father, give me the portion of goods that falleth to me. And he divided unto them his living. And not many days after the younger son gathered all together, and took his journey into a far country, and there wasted his substance with riotous living. And when he had spent all, there arose a mighty famine in that land; and he began to be in want. And he went and joined himself to a citizen of that country; and he sent him into his fields to feed swine. And he would fain have filled his belly with the husks that the swine did eat: and no man gave unto him. And when he came to himself, he said, How many hired servants of my father's have bread enough and to spare, and I perish with hunger! I will arise and go to my father, and will say unto him, Father, I have sinned against heaven, and before thee, And am no more worthy to be called thy son: make me as one of thy hired servants. And he arose and came to his father. But when he was yet a great way off, his father saw him, and had compassion, and ran, and fell on his neck, and kissed him.*

As long as the boy's consciousness was inferior, his father could not force him into a king's reality; his consciousness wouldn't allow it. He initially left home thinking like a boy but he returned thinking like a man. After he left home and escaped the safety and comforts of boyhood, he returned with a great appreciation of these things. He went from wealth to homelessness and returned to wealth and the only thing that changed was his perspective. He returned home consciously.

When I was inferior in my thinking, I did not value faithfulness in a relationship. As a consequence, my broken consciousness fractured the hearts of many women. When I evolved into consciousness, my priorities and values shifted. A conscious king thinks differently about God, about family, about money, about women and about fidelity (faithfulness). Faithfulness is a chief value of a conscious man.

Consciousness Speaks to the Man's Obvious Mind-Set and His Subconscious Beliefs.

Every man has a particular mind-set that guides his behavior. A part of that mind-set is front and center, but the greatest part of this mind-set is subliminal or subconscious. It is a man's subconscious mind-set that continuously sabotages his good intentions or maintains his honorable character.

There are the thoughts you think about and then there are the thoughts buried deep within your spirit (subconscious) that guide your life without effort or conscious thought.

For instance, a man may initially have to constantly think about being faithful to his wife. As he grows in his consciousness the idea of cheating becomes a foreign concept to his new consciousness. This brings the man to a place where he's not even tempted anymore, where he once struggled severely.

When the Mind-Set Shifts, Everything Recalibrates.

Look at the popular phrase "mind-set." We all have a mind-set. The question is: Who set our minds as men? The answers to this question are really too numerous to even attempt to list entirely, but here are a few for your consideration.

As children we parrot what we were taught; as men we are to consciously choose our thoughts, which influences our behavior.

Most Men Were Not Taught Right from Wrong, in Boyhood. Most Men Didn't Even See a Decent Example of a Man, Not Even in Their Fathers.

From the poor to no example of manhood, most men simply adopt a broken consciousness as a constitution for manhood. Our manhood was retarded by the poor examples that paraded before us.

Another societal factor in establishing a broken mind-set in men is the emphasis on *machismo*. Machismo is an attitude, quality, or way of behaving that agrees with traditional ideas about men being strong, highly sexual, flamboyant and aggressive. Machismo is driven by the male ego and male chauvinism (sexism).

Believe it or not, the church often adopts these narrow-minded and archaic views of manhood as biblically based. I find no real biblical basis for this toxic view of manhood. A man has to be more than muscle and sex. Also, manhood cannot be the subjugation of the very woman that God gave to us to help us succeed. These views are worldly and driven by grown boys who have not truly awakened to consciousness. The fact is this: most men have grown muscular and hairy bodies while functioning with the same adolescent pubescent mindset from decades ago. This is why the man malfunctions in his spiritual, societal and relational obligations. He's functioning with outdated software. He keeps crashing. He's like an iPhone that hasn't been updated in years.

A Man's Consciousness Must Surpass the Worldly Standards of Manhood. God Must Establish the Thinking.

The Word of God makes a powerful statement in Romans 12:1–3: *I beseech you therefore, brethren, by the mercies of God, that ye present your bodies a living sacrifice, holy, acceptable unto God, which is your reasonable service. And be not conformed to this world: but be ye transformed by the renewing of your mind, that ye may prove what is that good, and acceptable, and perfect, will of God. For I say, through the grace given unto me, to every man that is among you, not to think of himself more highly than he ought to think; but to think soberly, according as God hath dealt to every man the measure of faith.*

The message of this text is this: Be mindful not to allow your life to be shaped by worldly constraints and influences, but to be transformed by the renewing of your mind. The mind must be renewed by the Spirit of God and the Word of God. It is to the extent that the mind is intentionally renewed that the character aligns.

Character and Responsibility Are Driven by Consciousness. Your Conduct Will Never Rise Above Your Consciousness.

When I was a young man lacking consciousness, I couldn't be faithful, not even with people watching over me. I found a way to deceive and cheat, regardless. Now as a full-grown king-conscious man, I travel the world and I need no one to police me, for me to maintain my character.

A Man's Consciousness Is His Internal Government.

HOW TO FORM KING CONSCIOUSNESS

This is a very important question for us to answer. The fate of the current and future generations of men is resting on our ability to awaken men to who they are and why they exist. Our sons and mentees are looking to us for answers. How do we formulate king consciousness?

1. THE FOUNDATION OF CONSCIOUS THOUGHT STARTS IN WHAT WE WERE RAISED TO BELIEVE

What we were raised to believe about manhood forms our identity and values. We must take a real objective look at what we were raised to believe and measure those values by the Word of God and His view.

The Bible makes a very powerful statement about parenting and its importance in Proverbs 22:6, which says: *Train up a child in the way he should go: and when he is old, he will not depart from it.*

The quality of parenting has great weight in the outcome of the child. The seeds that were placed in us as children determine what eventually produces fruit in our lives. Most older men have not gotten, and younger men are not getting, the proper impartation at childhood.

Practically Everything We Are in Adulthood Started at Some Point in Our Boyhood.

For instance: The man who abuses women usually saw other men abuse women when he was a kid. He either witnessed his father abuse his mother or saw his uncles and brothers abuse women. The adult man who wastes his money on cars he can't afford and trinkets that don't make sense usually saw the adult males in his life practice financial irresponsibility and recklessness. The man who has no desire to be faithful has developed this mind-set since childhood as he watched the men in his life constantly cheat on their wives and girlfriends.

Conscious Thought Is the Result of the Words Spoken Over Your Life Constantly.

We are prophetic beings. What we say will find a way to materialize. To some great extent, all of us are either the beneficiaries of positive and affirming words spoken over us or we are the victims of negative professions.

The Bible says, in Proverbs 18:21: *Death and life are in the power of the tongue: and they that love it shall eat the fruit thereof.* If you were to paraphrase this verse it might sound like this: "Whatever you love to speak is what you will surely see manifested." Think about the negative or positive words spoken over your life that you are presently living up to.

> A Boy Is a Man in Seed Form. The Words Spoken Over His Life Will Promote Development or Stagnation.

As parents, mentors and leaders we must intentionally speak into the lives of boys, as it relates to who they are to be, before they can even respond to their potential. We must highlight their gifts and cultivate their potential as we coach them into the best version of themselves. Our words should encourage their highest aspirations and character.

> Boys Do Not Have Any Self-Confidence; Their Self-Confidence Is the Result of Their Community Having Confidence for Them.

If someone who loves the young man does not direct his consciousness, the world will misdirect him. The world will give him a false definition. A false definition always leads to poor character.

In the Old Testament, the family and community named their sons based on purpose and personal definition. Who he was, was instilled into him from birth. He was named intentionally.

For instance, in Matthew 1:21 it states: *And she shall bring forth a son, and thou shalt call his name Jesus:*

for he shall save his people from their sins. Jesus was named based on purpose and expectation. His family and community spoke life into his God-ordained potential and purpose.

It's very important to use intentional and empowering language in raising kings. When God put Adam in the garden, he told him what he should do and what he shouldn't do. Adam got his sense of identity from his father God.

> Most People Raise Grown Boys Because They Don't Understand That They Are Raising Men from the Start. A Boy Is Simply a Man-Child.

In the Jewish faith the father makes the son a man through words; they call it "the blessing." It's where the father tells the son who he is and what he will do in life. He also tells him what Jehovah will do for him if he serves him.

With all of this said, let me ask you a question: Who spoke over you, and what did they speak?

> Whoever Spoke Over Your Life Established Your Limitations.

2. THE SECOND LEVEL OF CONSCIOUSNESS IS IN WHAT WE ARE CONSISTENTLY EXPOSED TO

If a boy saw his father love his mother and provide for his family, that becomes his reality. If he sees men who play and hurt everybody in their path, that is then his reality.

Getting back to my testimony, I became a womanizer because early in my life as a child I was exposed to a sexual situation with older women. It was supposed to be a safe environment, but it became abusive. My parents were working multiple jobs to provide for our home. I was left in the care of a relative who seemed to be safe and responsible. Instead I was sexualized by older girls, which awakened something in me that would be a beast to control.

Before I had any grasp on right or wrong, I was locked into a mind-set that misshaped my life for decades. I was sexualized before I could even spell the word. That encounter awakened a spirit of perversion in me that would dominate my life for many years. When you think about it, what vice do you have in your life right now that you can trace back to something that started in childhood?

The challenge with exposure is that in the formative years, our exposure is determined by the choices of others; by the time we are grown and can make our own choices, we are already preconditioned to maintain the same comfort zones we were exposed to.

> It's Difficult to Be What You Didn't See; and It's Hard Not to Model and Perpetuate What You've Seen in Abundance.

The Bible lays it out plainly in 1 Kings 15:3: *And he walked in all the sins of his father, which he had done before him: and his heart was not perfect with the Lord his God, as the heart of David his father.*

A great deal of what we know as generational curses are generational exposure. We simply do what we've seen, as men. We become the same person as our ancestor in another body and generation. It's not an exact science, but it's quite often on point. The same vices that the grandfather had finds a way into the behavior of the sons and grandsons.

One day I looked at my life and I realized that I was a carbon copy of many of the men in my family. They had all of the women in the world, so to speak, but no credibility. They couldn't make their families work. They were not respected, and they had no future. I had to make a choice to rise above the limitations of my exposure. I had to become different to do something different. I started with choosing a different caliber of men to focus on. I thank God that my very own father had also broken the family curse and became my chief example of manhood.

When you come of age and you become consciously aware of who you are as a man, you must revisit your circle of influence. Put men before you who model the best in life. Purge your soul of the past foolery and nonsense.

One of the First Steps Towards Self-Actualization as a Man Lies in Making a Choice to Expose Yourself to More.

The wisdom of King Solomon, as it is found in Proverbs 13:20, states: *He that walketh with wise men shall be wise: but a companion of fools shall be destroyed.* A major part of your responsibility to yourself as a grown man is to choose who will influence you. As a child you had no choice in the matter, but now you must choose your level of exposure.

Fill your life with godly men who honor their word, serve their families and respect their money. Choose a better model of manhood to guide you. Choose something different than the dysfunctional examples of your childhood.

When We Expose Ourselves to the Opposite of the Broken and Dysfunctional Examples of Our Past, It Breaks the Stronghold.

3. THE THIRD FACTOR THAT ESTABLISHES CONSCIOUS THINKING IS IN WHAT OUR ENVIRONMENT EXPECTS OF US

Your personal standard is shifted when you intentionally elevate your environment. When you change your circle, the environment you are in as a man serves as a constant factor in your new consciousness. Kings run with kings.

Once again, King Solomon delivers a priceless pearl of wisdom in Proverbs 27:17. He says: *Iron sharpeneth iron; so a man sharpeneth the countenance of his friend.*

When a man shifts into king consciousness, he no longer settles for circles or environments that do not challenge him and make him better. Kings recognize the value of accountability and environments that demand more.

CHAPTER 3

THINGS THAT RUIN KINGS
Things That Will Destroy a Man's Greatness

We don't have to search hard or long to find men who had greatness draped over their lives and somehow found ways to squander it. There is no worse feeling in the world than underachieving. The question is: What ruins the greatness of a king? What destroys a king's rule and fractures his kingdom? What are the things that may dim the bulb of a man's bright future and diminish him to a fraction of his potential?

There's an interesting passage tucked away in the Bible. It is the account of a mother who teaches her son the ways of kings.

Her wisdom is found in Proverbs 1:8–9, which says: *My son, hear the instruction of thy father, and forsake not the law of thy mother: For they shall be an ornament of grace unto thy head, and chains about thy neck.*

The cultural implication surrounding this passage is that the father would speak instructions to the son, in passing, but the mother nurtured the son on a daily basis. The prince spent more time with his mother, the queen, than he did with his father, the king.

Proverbs 1:8, in the Message version, puts it this way: *Pay close attention, friend, to what your father tells you; never forget what you learned at your mother's knee.*

I found it interesting to read a text that supports the idea that kings and men may be trained to some extent by their mothers. Quite honestly, some of the soundest advice I have ever received as a man came from my mother. My mother was always the advocate for my becoming a faithful and honest man. My mother foresaw the destruction my loose lifestyle would bring. My mother identified my wife, Lisa, and endorsed her. There's something to be said about the positive impact a mother may have on the development of a man.

In the same token, we must address the fact that there are many men today whose development and growth have been retarded by toxic motherhood.

Toxic Motherhood Is When a Mother Refuses to Allow a Young Man to Grow Up and Face His Own Responsibility. She Shelters Him Until He Begins to Believe He Is Entitled to Be Kept and Cared For.

This broken consciousness spills over into his concepts of dating and marriage. Because his mother coddled him and catered to his every need, he now feels that all women in his life should spoil him.

Toxic Motherhood Is One of the Major Factors in the Broken Consciousness of Men Today.

This is especially significant when a young man has been raised by a single mother. When there is little to no male influence, it behooves the mother to raise her son intentionally. Sometimes mothers get caught in the trap of feeling sorry that their boys do not have a man around. As a response they attempt to make their boys feel better by going overboard to please them and to make life easy for them. Meaning well, they don't realize that this only handicaps the young man in the future. When he's called upon to respond as a man, he will have no muscle memory because his mother never allowed him to develop as a man.

The Overbearing Love of Mothers Has Often Canceled the Rise of Kings.

On another note, there is a biblical mother who did quite the opposite with her son; she taught him some of the things that would destroy kings. She gave her son sound wisdom and counsel. She made him responsible for his choices in life and made it clear to him that kings rise or fall based on the quality of their own choices in life.

The story is found in Proverbs 31:1–9 and reads: *The words of king Lemuel, the prophecy that his mother taught him. What, my son? and what, the son of my womb? and what, the son of my vows? Give not thy strength unto women, nor thy ways to that which destroyeth kings. It is not for kings, O Lemuel, it is not for kings to drink wine; nor for princes strong drink: Lest they drink, and forget the law, and pervert the judgment of any of the afflicted. Give strong drink unto him that is ready to perish, and wine unto those that be of heavy hearts. Let him drink, and forget his poverty, and remember his misery no more. Open thy mouth for the dumb in the cause of all such as are appointed to destruction. Open thy mouth, judge righteously, and plead the cause of the poor and needy.*

This is a very captivating scene. This is a king that is remembering the lessons his mother taught him about how to be and how not to be a king. The lesson is packed full of principles relative to life and manhood.

THINGS THAT DESTROY KINGS

When we analyze the context of the mother's instruction to King Lemuel there are a few things we gather. She insisted that these things are what destroy kings.

1. DON'T ENGAGE IN FRIVOLOUS SEXUALITY

The first principle we gather from the recollection of his mother's teaching is found in Proverbs 31:3, where it states: *Give not thy strength unto women, nor thy ways to that which destroyeth kings.*

According to the Complete Word Study Bible, the term "strength" comes from the Hebrew word *hayil*: It's a noun meaning *physical strength, wealth, and/or influence.*

The giving of one's strength is also a common reference to a man's sexual activity and the strength he loses when he encounters a woman sexually. This is the same reason boxers are prohibited to engage sexually before their fights: it is said to rob them of the strength in their legs.

His mother's first admonishment to him is to refrain from casual and pointless sexual encounters with women who do not factor into God's plan for his life and future. She is holding him accountable to manage himself in an area where weak men fail.

The one thing that will always draw a line between the men and the boys is sexual discipline.

The Word of God states, in 2 Timothy 2:22: *Flee also youthful lusts: but follow righteousness, faith, charity, peace, with them that call on the Lord out of a pure heart.* There's a lust that accompanies immaturity that should not be associated with a man of distinction and maturity. It is one thing for a teenager to be driven by sexual passions; it is another thing altogether for a man of responsibility to be irresponsible and careless.

There's always a judgment attached to sexual perversion and indiscretion. A man who does not control his passions will consistently fall short of the mark.

When a Man Cannot Manage His Sexuality, He Cripples His Destiny.

The Bible is full of examples of men whose sexual indiscretions left an asterisk by their names. Samson was blinded and died as a slave, because of Delilah. Solomon was the wisest king to ever live, yet he lived like a fool in his personal life. He was completely out of control when it came down to his sexual appetites. He literally had women from around the world. I always jokingly call Solomon the first international "player." David, who was Solomon's father, actually fell to becoming the chief conspirator in the murder of an innocent man, all because of his lust for that man's wife. David was having an adulterous affair with the woman and they conceived a child. David initially tried to blame the pregnancy on the woman's husband, but the man had not slept with his wife. David had him killed and then married the man's wife. Wow! This is deep stuff.

However, we do not have to go back into biblical texts to discover men who were diminished by unbridled sexual passion. We may look through contemporary history to find any number of great men who were belittled by their own inability to control their sexuality.

What makes it even more challenging for the man is when he is surrounded by women who are intentionally tempting him to fall. Many men experience hard times because of their appetite for easy women.

An Easy Woman Is the Carrier of Hard Times; and a Cheap Woman Will Cost You Your Future.

The Bible puts it very vividly in Proverbs 6:26, which states: *For by means of a whorish woman a man is brought to a piece of bread: and the adulteress will hunt for the precious life.*

There are certain women who are assigned to distract and destroy a man's destiny. If a man does not master himself, he will be a slave to demonic relationships that will leave him broken and empty. It will be in the latter years of a man's life that he may realize what he's traded for his destiny. A man does not need any woman; a man needs the woman who is ordained by God for his life. A king needs a queen.

The Right Woman Will Be a Man's Greatest Blessing, and the Wrong Woman Will Be His Greatest Curse.

PRACTICAL REASONS MEN FALL INTO SEXUAL TRAPS

A. He Has a Sexually Abusive Background.

Some men are actually victims of sexual abuse and their current indiscretions are the reflection of the pain they have been formed in. A man may assume a persona of sexual conquest to override his insecurity about molestation. Sometimes we use sexuality to cover the wounds we do not want to address.

B. He Is an Egomaniac Given to Flattery.

When a man's ego is inflated and not God-centered, he will be given over to the spirit of flattery and lust. He feeds his ego through his sexuality.

C. He Has a Faulty Idea of Manhood.

Many men are diminished to a level where they view the entirety of their manhood as length, girth and minutes. In other words, a man is no more than the size of his organ and his sexual performance stats. It's sad.

THE DANGERS OF A MAN'S SEXUAL INDISCRETIONS

A. He Creates Broken Relationships.

The first consequence of sexual indiscretion in a man's life is that it destroys ordained relationships. A man's sexual failures will destroy marriages and create father wounds. It will cause him to fail his sons and daughters as a father.

The Bible records, in Genesis 21:14–15: *And Abraham rose up early in the morning, and took bread, and a bottle of water, and gave it unto Hagar, putting it on her shoulder, and the child, and sent her away: and she departed, and wandered in the wilderness of Beer-sheba. And the water was spent in the bottle, and she cast the child under one of the shrubs.*

The back story is that Abraham conceived a child with his wife's slave, whose name was Hagar. Abraham disobeyed the exact will of God to create something on his own. When Abraham was done, it created confusion. He ultimately had to send his son, Ishmael, and his mother away. Sexual disorder always results in broken relationships.

B. He Damages the Innocence of Women.

When a Man Is Out of Control Sexually, He Destroys Women Physically and Emotionally.

In 2 Samuel 13:11–14, we see a horrible depiction of how far the damage of a man's lust can take him, and how it breaks the women in his life. It's actually an account of a brother taking advantage of his own sister.

The Bible says, in 2 Samuel 13:11–14: *And when she had brought them unto him to eat, he took hold of her, and said unto her, Come lie with me, my sister. And she answered him, Nay, my brother, do not force me; for no such thing ought to be done in Israel: do not thou this folly. And I, whither shall I cause my shame to go? and as for thee, thou shalt be as one of the fools in Israel. Now therefore, I pray thee, speak unto the king; for he will not withhold me from thee. Howbeit he would not hearken unto her voice: but, being stronger than she, forced her, and lay with her.*

This young man actually raped his own sister. A man's broken sexuality is the destruction of generations of women. We cannot afford to be the enemies of women.

C. He Loses His Reputation.

A man who cannot control his sexual impulses will never avoid the loss of reputation. He will be disrespected and ultimately disregarded as a jester. He will never be fit for great leadership because his reputation will constantly interfere with God's plan for him.

The Bible says, in Proverbs 22:1: *A good name is rather to be chosen than great riches, and loving favour rather than silver and gold.*
Kings always protect their names.

D. He Breaks His Connection to God.

The record of Samson is that he forfeited his ideal fellowship with God and lost his anointing. All of this happened because of his lust for Delilah. In Judges 16:20–21, it is recorded: *And she said, The Philistines be upon thee, Samson. And he awoke out of his sleep, and said, I will go out as at other times before, and shake myself. And he knew not that the Lord was departed from him. (verse 21) But the Philistines took him, and put out his eyes, and brought him down to Gaza, and bound him with fetters of brass; and he did grind in the prison house.*

He lost his sight, his strength and his purpose because of a woman. When he dishonored God, he lost everything. Sleeping around with women is more than sex; it may be your life.

E. He Creates Generational Curses Over His Kids.

Society is filled with examples of how the sexual improprieties of men creates a social domino effect. We can see the impact manifesting in the condition of the next generation. Our sons will tend to repeat our lawless behavior in their relationships and our daughters will quite often fail to locate the self-esteem they should have as women. These are things that may be laid to our charge when we fail to master ourselves as men.

There's a powerful text recorded in 1 Kings 15:3, which says: *And, he walked in all the sins of his father, which he had done before him: and his heart was not perfect with the Lord his God, as the heart of David his father.*

The poignant emphasis of this text is that the king's son continued the flawed behavior of his father that he witnessed. Our children are witnessing more than we may be aware of. We train our kids by our behavior much more than we do by our words.

F. He Develops Soul Ties with Unauthorized People.

A man does not always realize the total impact his actions are having on him. Sometimes we are deceived to think that we are simply playing a game. The reality is that we are involved in a very real situation with very harsh consequences. The spiritual implications of sexual perversion are weightier than most can imagine. Sexual immorality creates a bond between the man and those he encounters; it's called a "soul tie." The Bible says, in 1 Corinthians 6:16: *What? know ye not that he which is joined to an harlot is one body? for two, saith he, shall be one flesh.*

This was a difficult awakening of mine. I had lived a sexually loose and careless life for many years. I slept with every woman I could. As far as I was concerned, I was the master of the game.

Finally, the day came when I grew up and wanted to live a morally consistent life. I had my mind made up to abstain from any sexual impurity. All of a sudden, reality set in. I was like a junkie; I was addicted to these women. Freedom wasn't as easy as making a choice. I had to be set free from the consequences of my own choices.

HOW DOES A KING CONTROL HIS SEXUAL IMPULSES?

You will never turn off your sexual desire as a man. In fact, it's not about turning it off; it's about gaining control of your flesh. It would be like a person who overeats: they don't need to stop eating; they need to control their diet.

For a Man to Sanctify His Sex Life, It Will Require a Wise and Practical Approach to Living.

Listen to the wisdom of the psalms in Psalms 119:9–11, which says: *Wherewithal shall a young man cleanse his way? by taking heed thereto according to thy word. With my whole heart have I sought thee: O let me not wander from thy commandments. Thy word have I hid in mine heart, that I might not sin against thee.*

This process will require a total and complete investment of the man's body, soul and spirit into doing what pleases God. There are some practical steps that are required for a man to evolve.

YOU MUST MAKE PERSONAL GROWTH THE PRIORITY

Sexual indiscretion is a clear indication of spiritual and emotional immaturity. We can't change what we do until we address who we are.

You Cannot Do Better Until You Grow Better.

The Bible says, in 1 Corinthians 13:11: *When I was a child, I spake as a child, I understood as a child, I thought as* a child: but when I became a man, I put away childish things.

Emotional and Spiritual Maturity Are Not Automatic; They Are a Matter of Choice.

YOU MUST ELEVATE YOUR CIRCLE

Once you embrace the reality of a growth necessity, the next thing is to elevate the quality of the people you are associated with. In most cases, broken behavior mirrors the level of a man's company. The Bible says, in 1 Corinthians 15:33, in the Amplified version: *Do not be so deceived and misled! Evil companionships (communion, associations) corrupt and deprave good manners and morals and character.*

There's no mystery to my having fleas, if I'm living with dirty dogs. How many times do we see others or ourselves reflect the nature and misdeeds of those who are influencing us? We sound like them and walk like them because the people we associate with most leave imprints on our souls.

YOU MUST INTENTIONALLY DRAW CLOSER TO GOD

As we progress, we come to the point where we realize that we, alone, cannot control our carnal nature. We realize that we must have God. The Bible, in Galatians 5:16–17, in the Amplified version, says the following: *But I say, walk and live [habitually] in the [Holy] Spirit [responsive to and controlled and guided by the Spirit]; then you will certainly not gratify the cravings and desires of the flesh (of human nature without God). For the desires of the flesh are opposed to the [Holy] Spirit, and the [desires of the] Spirit are opposed to the flesh (godless human nature); for these are antagonistic to each other [continually withstanding and in conflict with each other], so that you are not free but are prevented from doing what you desire to do.*

At the end of the day, you are a man with all of the passions associated with being a man. You and I alike must have the very real presence of God to assist us to overcome ourselves.

Here's the hard-core truth: we don't need any outside influence to fall off the wagon sexually; it is in our base nature. This is why we must make it a point to live life in the presence of God and surrender to the Holy Spirit.

> We Can Only Overcome Ourselves by Giving Ourselves Over into the Hands of God through Prayer and Submission.

YOU CANNOT PUT CONFIDENCE IN YOUR FLESH

Once we've made our spiritual and emotional growth our priority, elevated our circle and drawn closer to God, we will definitely begin to feel the strength and see the victory manifesting in our lives. The common mistake is to begin to take credit for what God is doing.

> The Day a Man Takes Credit for Something God Is Doing, He's Destined to Fall.

You must always remember that the victory and freedom you're enjoying is not an indication of your goodness; it is a reflection of God's goodness and mercy towards you.

The Apostle Paul wrote to the Galatian Church and said, in Galatians 6:2–3: *Bear ye one another's burdens, and so fulfil the law of Christ. (verse 3) For if a man think himself to be something, when he is nothing, he deceiveth himself.*

Have you ever been around a person who thought they were better than they truly were? It's an embarrassing sight. You can just sit back and wait. You know that reality is going to return soon, and it won't be pretty.

YOU NEED MALE ACCOUNTABILITY IN YOUR LIFE

Every man needs good men who will hold him accountable to the higher standard. We all need accountability and a lot less enablement. The writer of Hebrews says the following, in Hebrews 10:24: *And let us consider one another to provoke unto love and to good works.*

> Who Do You Have in Your Life Who Will Hold You to a Righteous Standard Without Compromise?

2. DO NOT DEVELOP THE HABIT OF INTOXICATION

The second instruction the king's mother gave him was to avoid a life of intoxication. Her words are recorded in Proverbs 31:4, which says: *It is not for kings, O Lemuel, it is not for kings to drink wine; nor for princes strong drink: (verse 5) Lest they drink, and forget the law, and pervert the judgment of any of the afflicted.*

Intoxication usually refers to living under the influence of some mind-altering substance. Alcohol and drugs are widely used to separate a person from their consciousness. Many people are living such depressed lives that they must medicate to exist.

One of the sad consequences of the broken consciousness that male chauvinism and the machismo culture have produced is the glorification of drugs and alcohol as a rite of passage for young men. This is always a reflection of an immature spirit. A man who is conscious of his responsibility values his ability to respond. He cannot effectively do that when he is intoxicated.

Kings Must Always Be About Their Wits.

The Bible puts it so plainly in Proverbs 20:1, which states: *Wine is a mocker, strong drink is raging: and whosoever is deceived thereby is not wise.*

This is not an argument against the consumption of alcohol. Every adult person will have to make a decision for or against it. It is, however, an argument against drunkenness. It is never wise to be under the influence of any substance, as a king. There's always too much at stake.

Stimulants Poison the Body, Distract the Focus and Pervert the Judgment.

How many men have lost their lives because they had too much to drink and committed vehicular homicide? How many men have done foolish deeds because of the impact of marijuana or drugs?

A King Must Be Sober-Minded and Always in Full Control of His Judgment.

Imagine the potential for destruction when a man who possesses great power is not truly in possession of his own faculties. When that man is inebriated, he is simultaneously rendered vulnerable amidst a suspect society seeking to take advantage of the powerful. His lack of discipline may prove to be highly volatile to himself, his family and his destiny.

Bad People Will Always Use the Power of a Drunk King.

There's a king by the name of Herod who was so drunk with lust that he promised a young woman anything she desired if she would do a sensual dance for him. She did the dance, and when she was done, she asked him to execute John the Baptist and to give her his head. She was being controlled by her mother, but she used the king's drunken lust to manipulate his power.

The story is recorded in Matthew 14:6–11: *But when Herod's birthday was kept, the daughter of Herodias danced before them, and pleased Herod. Whereupon he promised with an oath to give her whatsoever she would ask. And she, being before instructed of her mother, said, Give me here John Baptist's head in a charger. And the king was sorry: nevertheless for the oath's sake, and them which sat with him at meat, he commanded it to be given her. And he sent, and beheaded John in the prison. And his head was brought in a charger and given to the damsel: and she brought it to her mother.*

The king was managed by his own lack of sobriety.

The king's mother clarifies why it is important for him, as king, to maintain a level head. She tells him that a king is responsible for the well-being of others and cannot afford to be out of touch.

The text in Proverbs 31:9 says: *Open thy mouth, judge righteously, and plead the cause of the poor and needy.*

A king-conscious man understands that God gives affluence and influence to a man to elevate those in life who have neither. Kings do not squander their favor and opportunities on pointless self-indulging activities. Kings live to make a mark.

Kings Live for Legacy, and Legacy Is Always in What One's Life Meant to Others.

Don't get drunk on power and forget that the best use of power is to serve others.

Jesus said, in Matthew 23:11–12: *But he that is greatest among you shall be your servant. And whosoever shall exalt himself shall be abased; and he that shall humble himself shall be exalted.*

When you plead for the voiceless, you retain the favor of God.

CHAPTER 4

UNDERSTANDING THE TENSION BETWEEN KINGS AND QUEENS

The Spiritual and Social Complexities between Men and Women

The most telling aspect of a king-conscious man is the approach he takes with women. A real man always manages relationships with women honorably. This value is consistent, from his relationship with his mother, to that of his sisters, his friends, and his girlfriends, and absolutely with his wife.

A King-Conscious Man Will Adore His Queen.

The king-conscious man views the woman as God's gift to him. He does not see her as his competition or opponent; he views her as a precious gift. One of the clearest indicators of a man's arrested development is his perception of women.

The Greatest Mark of Manhood Is Revealed in the Man's Attitude Towards Womanhood.

The woman must be accepted and respected as the man's partner in success. Any smidgen of bias or disrespect for the woman will certainly handicap the man's capacity.

When we observe the game of chess, we can see the revelation of the queen's value. On the chessboard, the queen is the most prolific player, and her entire agenda is to protect the king. Usually, when the king loses his queen, he is doomed. It takes a miracle for a player to survive the loss of his queen, unless he's playing a miserably inept opponent. The queen has limitless ability and all of it is employed to defend and advance the king.

The King's MVP (Most Valuable Player) Is His Queen.

In the game of life, a wise king understands the value of his queen and he guards her intentionally and wisely. He respects and honors her for her contribution to the kingdom. Where would we be without women?

With all of this being said, the fact remains that men and women tend to have a natural tension, and it often disrupts the potential for harmony. It's not uncommon to find a man and a woman who love each other endlessly, but who never seem to get along. An uneasiness seems to camp out in the midst of a relationship that creates an unwelcome rivalry and power struggle.

It takes a true king to understand these facts and to apply wisdom during the moment to overcome the rift. Kings possess a level of understanding that transcends the typical man. Kings know how to harmonize with their queens.

The scripture declares, in 1 Peter 3:7: *Likewise, ye husbands, dwell with them according to knowledge, giving honour unto the wife, as unto the weaker vessel, and as being heirs together of the grace of life; that your prayers be not hindered.*

Notice, the admonishment is for the man to dwell with his wife according to knowledge. A man must possess a deep knowledge of himself and an understanding of the woman in his life to maintain harmony in the relationship. Society breeds a tension and confusion between men and women. The fastest way to dismantle a kingdom is to divide the king and queen over assumptions and insecurities.

There Are Spiritual and Social Complexities Between Men and Women That Feed the Tension.

A major aspect of a man truly ruling as a king in society is revealed in how he respects and honors the queen. True kings perceive and respect the necessity of queens. After all, it was God who said, "It is not good for man to be alone." From that point, God created woman to help man.

This is found in Genesis 2:18, where it states: *And the Lord God said, it is not good that the man should be alone; I will make him an help meet for him.*

The woman is created and generated by God to help the man. Society works tirelessly to diminish women's usefulness in the minds of men. For instance, if we would take our cue from media and entertainment, the woman is nothing more than a sexual tool. If we take our signal from the archaic religions of the world, the woman is merely a subordinate in servitude. If one were to ask the fashion industry, she is just something pretty to look at. The reality is, the woman is more than all of these assumptions. The woman is the queen.

> The Woman Is Not a Sex Toy or a Plaything. The Woman Is a Necessity to the Man and Dominion.

One day, while on the internet, I heard a profound perspective on the woman's relationship to the man. The statement was made by Minister Louis Farrakhan. He said, in a particular video, "A man does not know the true extent of his development as a man without a woman because the woman is designed to test and to verify his manhood." He explained, "A real woman will test the man, because she has to know that he will stand up for her and their children." Wow! When I heard that, it resonated with my spirit. A part of the tension is the testing. The woman is testing the man's worthiness, even when she's unaware that this is what she is doing.

I understood what he was saying, because I have been in the process of manhood for a long time, and I know the importance of strong women in the development of the man. A weak woman does nothing for a king's development. Weak women do more to stagnate the process of manhood than anything. Weak women are the enablers of indecisive and inept men. Strong women are the architects of kings.

So, the tension between strong men and strong women is purposeful and understandable. There's a method to the madness, as some might say.

THE LOVE-HATE DYNAMIC

With all of the purpose and favor set upon the covenant between men and women, there is a tension that is present within the relationship. For a man, it takes wisdom and experience to cut through the trial and error and to understand the backstory of the clash. Why can't men and women live without each other and why can they rarely live together without drama? What is it? We are exclusive partners in dominion and yet we function like chief enemies most of the time. Where did this start?

HOW THE BATTLE OF THE KINGS AND QUEENS BEGAN

It all started shortly after the genesis (beginning). In the beginning, God's original decree was for Adam and Eve to operate in joint dominion. It was a co-dominion system. Adam and Eve were king and queen of God's earthly creation.

Misogynistic theology and male chauvinistic perspectives will have us believe that Eve was created as being inferior to Adam. You might be led to think that Eve was in servitude. Not so.

The Word of God actually states, in Genesis 1:27–28: *So God created man in his own image, in the image of God created he him; male and female created he them. And God blessed them, and God said unto them, Be fruitful, and multiply, and replenish the earth, and subdue it: and have dominion over the fish of the sea, and over the fowl of the air, and over every living thing that moveth upon the earth.*

Notice how God blessed "them" and commissioned "them" to be fruitful, multiply and dominate. Eve was Adam's co-equal in dominion. It is a major error to envision the woman as anything other than an equal to the man. God's original order, for man and woman, was for them to be co-equals.

God Never Assigned Either to Dominate the Other.

Of course, Adam was the first created, and God held him responsible for maintaining the agreement God made with him about not eating of the fruit of the tree. God created Adam and blessed him with everything he could imagine. The only thing God required from Adam was obedience. God said to Adam, "You may eat freely, just do not touch this particular tree." This is where we get the idea of the apple from. All Adam had to do was comply.

God's deal with Adam is recorded in Genesis 2:17, where it states: *And the Lord God commanded the man, saying, Of every tree of the garden thou mayest freely eat: But of the tree of the knowledge of good and evil, thou shalt not eat of it: for in the day that thou eatest thereof thou shalt surely die.*

Though the covenant was between God and Adam, once Eve was created, they functioned as co-equals. Think about it: If Adam didn't view Eve as an equal, why would he have even considered her suggestion, when she asked him to eat of the fruit? He considered it because he respected her as an equal. They had a co-equal culture.

God gave Adam an order to dominate everything else, but he never gave him the idea to dominate Eve. Prior to Adam falling into sin and disobeying God, he never was instructed to assume authority over the woman, Eve. They were living in dominion together.

Adam's Disobedience Was the Interruption of Their Dominion.

The interesting thing about the entire account of Adam and Eve's fall from dominion was how it transpired. God did not take action against them when Eve ate of the fruit, but God stepped in quickly with judgment when Adam disobeyed.

The Bible says, in Genesis 3:6–7: *And when the woman saw that the tree was good for food, and that it was pleasant to the eyes, and a tree to be desired to make one wise, she took of the fruit thereof, and did eat, and gave also unto her husband with her; and he did eat. And the eyes of them both were opened, and they knew that they were naked; and they sewed fig leaves together and made themselves aprons.*

When Adam Participated in the Disobedience, the Innocence of Dominion Lifted.

Adam's covenant with God protected them from darkness. As long as Adam was in sync with the will of God, all was well. Adam represented the protection of the woman; when Adam got out of order, he exposed the entire union, and immediately God came looking for Adam to reckon with them.

When Adam Disobeyed God, He Exposed Eve Through His Actions.

In Genesis 3:9–11, it says: *And the Lord God called unto Adam, and said unto him, Where art thou? And he said, I heard thy voice in the garden, and I was afraid, because I was naked; and I hid myself. And he said, Who told thee that thou wast naked? Hast thou eaten of the tree, whereof I commanded thee that thou shouldest not eat?*

We see here how God held Adam responsible for the transgression. God would later deal with Eve, but nothing shifted until Adam got out of order.

Though they were co-equals in dominion, they each had specific responsibilities. We could liken it to co-pilots of the same plane. Both pilots have, to some extent, the same abilities, but different authority and responsibilities based on their positions. The level of authority also changes the level of liability. If a plane flight goes wrong, the media will discuss the pilot of the craft. They won't be too interested in the performance of the co-pilot. Likewise, when things went off track in Eden, God came searching for Adam, the pilot.

DOMINION LOST

It is after Adam's massive blunder that we begin to see the dysfunction enter into the relationship between Adam and Eve. The disintegration of dominion becomes apparent after their transgressions. When they offended God, they disrupted their place of dominion.

After "the Fall," God began to dole out punishments for their individual disobedience. God told Adam that he would now earn a living by the sweat of his brow through hard labor. To the serpent (Satan) he said, "You will crawl on your belly eating the dust of the earth." As dramatic as the penalties for Adam and Satan were, it's when we look at the punishment pronounced upon Eve that we get insight into the post-dominion tension between the man and the woman.

The Bible says, in Genesis 3:16: *Unto the woman he said, I will greatly multiply thy sorrow and thy conception; in sorrow thou shalt bring forth children; and thy desire shall be to thy husband, and he shall rule over thee.*

It is here that we begin to witness the crisis between the king and queen when God is absent from the equation.

When God said to Adam, *the day you disobey and eat of the fruit, you shall surely die,* he was not talking about physical death only; he was also talking about spiritual death. Spiritual death is separation from the presence and influence of God. When Adam and Eve ate of the fruit, they exposed themselves spiritually. It was a spiritual nakedness they felt. They were trying to cover their bodies when the issue was that their souls had been exposed.

So, from this new reality of broken fellowship with God, we see this fractured king and queen come to terms with their unfortunate and dysfunctional predicament.

THE CURSE OF POST-DOMINION RELATIONSHIPS

There's a tremendous revelation in those few words spoken in Genesis 3:16, when God says to Eve, "Adam will now rule over you."

For the first time in creation, God tells Adam to exercise authority over Eve. This newfound authority of Adam's, over Eve, was a punishment for her disobedience. This indicates that in God's original and ideal design, Adam was not meant to rule Eve; Adam's ruling was only introduced as a punishment for Eve's transgression.

Adam Ruling Over Eve Was Not Only a Punishment to Eve; It Was Also a Punishment to Adam.

I know that statement is hard to process. How could being made the boss be a punishment? Think about it this way: millions of men are, unsuccessfully, trying to boss strong women. For generations we have tried, and it is all-consuming.

> It's So Hard to Manage a Strong Woman That Most Men Eventually Give Up Trying.

There's a reason that the woman is hard to manage. When God told Adam to rule over Eve, it was like assigning a person to rule an African lion. Imagine if someone pronounced you as the boss of the lion and dropped it off at your house and left. That's a dangerous undertaking. The nature and natural strength of the lion would not accommodate your rule.

We must remember that Eve was created as a dominator, which makes her impossible to rule. She was not created to be controlled. There's a natural resistance in a queen when she's being dominated.

Again, In Genesis 3:16, God says to Eve: *Your desire shall be to your husband and he shall rule over you.*

In certain theological circles this section of language is interpreted in this way: "Eve, you shall desire to have your husband's position and in spite of it he shall rule you." In other words, she will constantly work to usurp Adam's new authority.

Look at how Genesis 3:16 reads, in the English Standard version of the Bible: *To the woman he said, "I will surely multiply your pain in childbearing; in pain you shall bring forth children. Your desire shall be contrary to your husband, but he shall rule over you."*

Eve Works Against Adam Ruling Over Her Because It Is Not the Natural Order.

Here's where we begin to see the social implications of the post-dominion curse. If Adam is going to rule over Eve and Eve is going to fight against his authority because it's not in her nature to be ruled, Adam is going to have to "break" Eve.

Imagine the task: God tells Adam to rule Eve and God doesn't tweak Eve's temperament. She is still as dominion-minded as before. Adam is trying to control a being that is his equivalent. How can one control a lion? One must break the lion's spirit. One has to forcefully divorce it from its nature.

It was a punishment for Adam to rule Eve because being ruled was not in Eve's makeup. It was not in her nature.

THE BROKEN RIB

Little did Adam know the full fallout of the punishment for his actions. This post-dominion fallen state of humankind would come to a place where men would subjugate the spirit of the woman through intentional acts of abuse and control. As we can see today, many women have been broken into submission while many still resist.

It's amazing how the woman who came from the man's rib is now the target of the man's aggression. The woman he loves is the same woman he feels compelled to break. They are both rendered confused and perplexed because few have an understanding of what is going on between the king and the queen.

Many Men Have Degenerated into Abusers and Manipulators to Rule Over Women.

The rise in narcissism (extreme self-interest and an inability to feel empathy) is engineered through the celebration of misogyny. Everything from physical to sexual and emotional abuse can all be traced back to the breakdown between God, Adam and Eve. When Adam disturbed the spirit of dominion, he would start a downward cycle that has made men and women adversarial to each other.

Though they both, by nature, love each other, they have a propensity to clash. He's seeking to break her spirit while she's attempting to take his authority. The man and the woman are like two lions in a cage; there is really no winner.

THE NEW KINGDOM ORDER

Adam compromised the spirit of co-dominion when he disobeyed God and ushered in the punishments that would make man's relationship to woman at best very difficult; but, through Jesus Christ, there is a new order that reverses the curse and restores co-dominion.

The Bible states, in Romans 5:14–15: *Nevertheless death reigned from Adam to Moses, even over them that had not sinned after the similitude of Adam's transgression, who is the figure of him that was to come. But not as the offence, so also is the free gift. For if through the offence of one many be dead, much more the grace of God, and the gift by grace, which is by one man, Jesus Christ, hath abounded unto many.*

Without going into the deep theological and doctrinal depths of this passage, I will give you the gist. Just like Adam brought all men following him into his curse, Jesus Christ brings all men following him, through faith, into his blessing and grace. What we lost with Adam we may regain in Christ.

Adam squandered dominion. Adam forfeited dominion because dominion was a joint activity between Adam and Eve. Sin created a breach.

In Christ, the Man and the Woman May Return to the Place of Co-Dominion.

Generations of men who inherited the chaos Adam created have struggled with their relationships with the queens. We've evolved into monstrous figures in our attempts at ruling and controlling the queens. We have broken scores of women with our antics and tactics to subdue their spirit. This has proven to be acts of futility. It leaves us exhausted, the women broken and a cloud of misuse hovering over our consciousness as men.

The Question Is: How Do the Kings and Queens Co-Dominate Again?

There's a simple but profound wisdom that will solve the issues between the kings and the queens. Just like it all started and stopped with Adam in the beginning, so it is again; it starts with us as men.

Men who are not enlightened are still trying to rule the lion. In other words, men who lack this wisdom are yet attempting to manipulate and dominate women. This never works. It either leaves your woman broken and depleted or angry and rebellious. Either way, it's no recipe for dominion.

How Can a Man Rule a Lion?

A man may only rule a lion when the lion submits. A man may only lead a woman when the woman submits. Submission is not something that a man can force or enforce. If you are forcing submission, it's no longer submission; it's abuse. Submission is not something a man takes; it's something a woman freely gives to a deserving man.

The Word of God states, in 1 Peter 3:5–7: *For after this manner in the old time the holy women also, who trusted in God, adorned themselves, being in subjection unto their own husbands: Even as Sara obeyed Abraham, calling him lord: whose daughters ye are, as long as ye do well, and are not afraid with any amazement.*

Likewise, ye husbands, dwell with them according to knowledge, giving honour unto the wife, as unto the weaker vessel, and as being heirs together of the grace of life; that your prayers be not hindered.

Usually when we read text like this, as men, we zoom in on the wives-being-in-subjection part; we ignore the part where it talks about husbands being knowledgeable and demonstrating honor.

Submission Is a Fruit, While Honor Is the Seed. The Seed Must Precede the Fruit.

How does a king lead a queen? The simple but profound answer is honor. When we lead from a place of honor, we will cultivate the fruit of submission. When the men are honoring the women and the women are willingly submitting to the men, it is the return to dominion. It is when we understand the common objective without a need to dominate each other.

CHAPTER 5

KINGS ARE INTENTIONAL ABOUT RELATIONSHIPS

Kings Are Not Random or Irresponsible in Relationships

The wisest and wealthiest king of the Bible was Solomon. When Solomon took the throne, God asked him what he wanted. Imagine that. God asks you, "What do you want?" An immature man might have asked for a Rolls Royce, Rolex watch, mansion or bags filled with gold. The young king, Solomon, says, "Give me wisdom and discretion concerning people."

Solomon Prayed for Discretion and Wisdom to Judge His Relationships.

The story is recorded in 1 Kings 3:7–10, where it says: *And now, O Lord my God, thou hast made thy servant king instead of David my father: and I am but a little child: I know not how to go out or come in. And thy servant is in the midst of thy people which thou hast chosen, a great people, that cannot be numbered nor counted for multitude. Give therefore thy servant an understanding heart to judge thy people, that I may discern between good and bad: for who is able to judge this thy so great a people? And the speech pleased the Lord, that Solomon had asked this thing.*

The king prayed for wisdom to judge and to discern the people he was called to lead. Solomon was wise enough to know that people may attach to kings to hitchhike a ride on the king's influence. Most people are not what they appear to be. When kings do not discern the people around them, they are usually manipulated unawares. It's a pitiful king who allows his grace to be managed by his subjects.

Kings Have a Multitude of Decisions That Will Impact the Stability of the Kingdom; Knowing People Is Mandatory.

Please remember that we are using the terms "king" and "man" interchangeably, in this document. When we reference things pertaining to kings, we are referring to things pertaining to men. Just like King Solomon, every man must know the people he's connected to, and those attaching to him.

Solomon's prayer should heavily resonate with every man. Solomon asked God to give him an "understanding heart." Not only does a king discern people for the purposes of weeding out the pretenders, but he also seeks to sincerely understand the people within his gates.

Can you imagine how many families are busted, businesses destroyed and careers ended, all because a man did not seek to understand the people surrounding him?

When I look over my own life as a leader, there are many relationships that did not need to end. They ended because I, as the leader, was not wise enough, at the time, to seek an understanding of the people.

King-Conscious Men Always Seek Understanding.

The Holy Bible gives us a great pearl of wisdom. It's in Proverbs 4:7, which says: *Wisdom is the principal thing; therefore, get wisdom: and with all thy getting get understanding.*

Kings always seek to understand, over being understood. He who has the power must be the servant to he who has less. The only way a man seeks to understand others is if he knows himself first. Solomon could pray for the understanding of others, because he already knew who he was in God. His identity was secure.

When a Man Knows Who He Is and Is Secure in His Power and Position, He Seeks to Understand Those Whom He Has Oversight Of. Kings Rule with Empathy.

The previous statement alone challenges most of what we've been taught about being a man. Society makes us believe that ruling is about enforcing our selfish will upon everyone around us. As a consequence, we feed the narcissistic gene that tends to reside within the male psyche, and we destroy everything in our care, from women, to children, to friends, to coworkers, and even to sibling relationships. Most men fail to understand that a king is not a tyrant.

A King Is a Powerful Servant.

When a king fails to understand the people he's assigned to, he breeds rebellion and dysfunction.

For instance, there's another biblical king who did not seek to understand the people he was overseeing, and this produced calamity. In fact, this king was Solomon's son. Wisdom is not always generational or hereditary.

The record is found in 1 Kings 11:6–19. Due to the verbosity (wordiness) of the passage mentioned, I will tell you the story and trust you to read the Bible's account for yourself.

King Rehoboam succeeded his father, Solomon. He had the opportunity to seek the counsel of the older men who served with his father, or he could listen to the counsel of the young men who were his contemporaries.

When he went to the older men they said, "Listen to the people and make life easier for them. They will serve you for your entire life." He then went to the young, ambitious men and they said, "Threaten the people with hardship and force them to serve."

When it was all said and done, he chose the counsel of the young men. He did not seek to understand the people, and he functioned as a tyrant. The people rose in rebellion and ran Rehoboam off his throne and out of his kingdom. He lost the kingdom because he did not seek to understand his people.

He destroyed the kingdom and his rule forever.

When a Man Does Not Seek a Sincere Understanding of His People, He Sets Himself Up for Failure.

The husband who does not understand his wife is destined for a quarrelsome relationship. There's nothing to compare to a woman in rebellion. As fathers we must understand our children, to effectively guide them. This principle applies to the job, to the church, to friendships and to any other relationship. King-conscious men manage their relationships with understanding.

Isn't it amazing that a man's greatest complaint about his wife and kids is that he doesn't understand them? The reality is that most men never apply themselves to understanding them. We fall victim to the almost innate narcissism that is present within a culture of toxic masculinity, and we approach our relationships as tyrants and not as servants.

It Is a King's Responsibility to Know His People.

In reference to a man being a husband, the Bible gives some specific instruction in 1 Peter 3:7, where it says: *Likewise, ye husbands, dwell with them according to knowledge, giving honour unto the wife, as unto the weaker vessel, and as being heirs together of the grace of life; that your prayers be not hindered.*

The knowledge that the text is encouraging the husband to possess is largely attained through selfless observation of the wife's tendencies and needs.

The Old Testament Jewish tradition for husbands is quite interesting. In Deuteronomy 24:5, the new husbands were instructed: *...when a man hath taken a new wife, he shall not go out to war, neither shall he be charged with any business: but he shall be free at home one year, and shall cheer up his wife which he hath taken.*

The husband was directed to be free from war and business for twelve months, to get to know his wife.

A Man Gives Intentional Attention to the Things That Matter.

Even as far back as Adam in the garden, there's this revelation of the man getting to know the needs and tendencies of everything he was assigned to. It says, in Genesis 2:15: *And the Lord God took the man and put him into the garden of Eden to dress it and to keep it.*

When God gave him the responsibility of dressing it, it meant that he was to work and to serve his environment. Adam was as a servant king.

When it references Adam keeping it, it meant that he was to watch and guard it. The message is crystal clear: Adam was lord of the garden and servant to everything he was set over. A man who has no concept of serving and paying attention is not mature enough to rule.

The Foundation of Classical Manhood Is Selfless Service to Society.

The most precious of all of the man's assets are his relationships. God has made the man the guardian of the family, to prophetically guard in the natural and spiritual.

The First Man Diminished the Entirety of Mankind Because He Didn't Manage His Relationship with His Wife.

The account is found in Genesis 3:4–9, which says: *And the serpent said unto the woman, Ye shall not surely die: For God doth know that in the day ye eat thereof, then your eyes shall be opened, and ye shall be as gods, knowing good and evil. And when the woman saw that the tree was good for food, and that it was pleasant to the eyes, and a tree to be desired to make one wise, she took of the fruit thereof, and did eat, and gave also unto her husband with her; and he did eat. And the eyes of them both were opened, and they knew that they were naked; and they sewed fig leaves together, and made themselves aprons. And they heard the voice of the Lord God walking in the garden in the cool of the day: and Adam and his wife hid themselves from the presence of the Lord God amongst the trees of the garden. And the Lord God called unto Adam, and said unto him, Where art thou?*

Adam failed his responsibility to his wife. If he had assumed the role of leader, rather than becoming a following group thinker, he could have corrected his wife.

Eve Was the First Time We Saw a Woman with Broken Consciousness.

Satan deceived Eve into thinking that she needed to be more than she was. What he subconsciously convinced her of was that she was not enough. The reality was that she was the best version of womanhood. She had dominion over the very serpent that filled her mind with lies.

Who should have rescued her from this delusion? Adam should have, but he failed her.

HOW DID SATAN GAIN ACCESS TO EVE'S EAR?

Eve was somebody's wife; the man was present, and yet Satan deceived the man's wife. How? Adam's God-given responsibility was to guard and keep the garden; that included guarding his wife. Adam failed!

Notice that God did not come checking for Eve after things fell apart. God came looking for Adam. God holds the man responsible for guiding the woman.

The etymological origins of the term "husband" refer to one who manages and bands the house together. A husband is a "house-band." Adam's responsibility was to teach his wife the covenant. He allowed Satan to twist her understanding. From this, we may deduce that humankind's great problems started with Adam not fulfilling his role in his primary relationship. Adam was present and absent at the same time.

When Kings Fail in Their Relationships,
the Kingdom Suffers.

THE KING'S VITAL RELATIONSHIPS

1. A MAN'S RELATIONSHIP WITH GOD

A man is never complete without his connection to God. Even in the beginning Adam did not become vibrant until God breathed into him. I am certain that men from a diversity of spiritual levels and persuasions are reading this book. Let me help you at this point. When I talk about a man and his relationship to God, I am not referring to religion whatsoever. Sometimes the most anti-God factor is religion. There's a vast difference between religion and relationship. The reason we have so many corrupt brothers in the church is because they are pursuing religion apart from an authentic relationship with God. Religion cannot transform.

A Man Is Only Transformed by a Relationship with Christ.

What does it mean to have a relationship with Christ? The Apostle Paul addresses it with the Galatian Church.
    He says, in Galatians 2:20: *I am crucified with Christ: nevertheless, I live; yet not I, but Christ liveth in me: and the life which I now live in the flesh I live by the faith of the Son of God, who loved me, and gave himself for me.*
    When a man has a relationship with Christ, there is the internal presence of Christ in his spirit. God influences your mind and behavior from within. A religious man depends on the external restraints of religious rules and rituals to steer him. And even then, these have a fleeting effect.

> A Man Who Knows Christ Depends Less and Less on External Restraints. His Source of Self-Government Is the Internal Presence of God.

When a man's relationship is right with Christ, he is disciplined and controlled, even in private. He will not demand oversight or policing. Christ lives in him.

The obvious question, for some, might be: How do I get a relationship with Christ? I am so very glad that you asked. I will give you the skeleton model. There's a tremendous gulf between what we know as religion, versus "salvation." There are millions of people who are deeply enthralled in religion who have never been saved.

> To Be Saved, Simply Put, Means to Be Delivered from the Misery and Depravity of Having a Spiritual Separation from God.

When we use the term "lost," it means to be in a position where one lacks a connection to his creator. It does not speak of morality or character. To be lost is to be out of position. When we do not have fellowship with our creator, we are deficient in certain necessities like peace, joy, security and many other things that bring balance to life.

If you go back to the fall of Adam in the Bible, we see what this looks like. When Adam disobeyed God, he was disconnected from his creator. We saw how his entire demeanor and confidence as a man were shattered. Even the way he related to his wife was affected. Adam was "lost." He was detached from his essence (God).

When a man lacks this fundamental connection to God, he flounders. He searches for fulfillment in sex, money, power, achievements, physical dominance, emotional control of others and even false religions that appeal to his self-importance. He's "lost." He may not be a bad person; he's simply disconnected from his true source. In many cases he may even be a great guy, but without an authentic connection to God he lives with a deep sense of lack; something is missing. He's lost.

A Man Only Discovers Peace and True Fulfillment When He Closes the Gap Between Himself and His Creator.

There are many religions that spread their message as to how a man may close this gap. I am not a person who believes I need to build my position by attacking another man's. Truth always rises to the top and speaks for itself.

I will only share with you what I have found to close the gap for me. I was once a young man lost in religion. I was confused about how to bring peace to my heart. I wanted to find what would reconcile my heart to God. Jesus Christ did it for me. I was born in the church. I was the pastor's son and I never found myself until I actually formed a personal relationship with Jesus for myself.

When I Found Jesus, I Found Myself as a Man.

Getting "saved" is so simple that it's referred to as the ABCs of salvation. The A stands for "Admit." Admit that you are a sinner and that you've messed up. That means something different for all of us, but here is where it starts. The Bible says, in Romans 3:23: *For all have sinned, and come short of the glory of God.* You cannot get caught up in your pride and attempt to cover the truth about yourself. It begins with us saying, "I am a sinner. I'm not right. I need help."

The B stands for "Believe." After you admit your sins, believe in the Lord Jesus Christ as the savior. Jesus came to save sinners like you and me. Religion might make you believe that you have to jump through fifteen hoops; not so!

The Bible says, in John 3:16–17: *For God so loved the world, that he gave his only begotten Son, that **whosoever believeth in him should not perish, but have everlasting life**. For God sent not his Son into the world to condemn the world; but that the world through him might be saved.*

The C stands for "Confess." Once you have admitted your sins and believe in the Lord Jesus Christ, the final stage is to confess him as Lord of your life. The Word of God, in Romans 10:9–10, states: *That if thou shalt confess with thy mouth the Lord Jesus, and shalt believe in thine heart that God hath raised him from the dead, thou shalt be saved. For with the heart man believeth unto righteousness; and with the mouth confession is made unto salvation.*

If you will do these three things, sincerely, you will feel a shift in your heart. You will have ignited your relationship with the Lord Jesus. There will be a change in your spirit that will be undeniable. The only persons who may understand your spiritual experience will be those who have had the same experience.

A Man Must Intentionally Nurture His Relationship with God to Be Equipped to Lead. A Man Must Be Led to Lead.

There's a wonderful illustration of spiritual manhood depicted. It's when Jesus wanted to feed the hungry multitude. He instructed the disciples to make the men sit down. The provision for the family was flowing through the obedience of the men.

The Bible says, in John 6:10–12: *And Jesus said, Make the men sit down. Now there was much grass in the place. So the men sat down, in number about five thousand. And Jesus took the loaves; and when he had given thanks, he distributed to the disciples, and the disciples to them that were set down; and likewise of the fishes as much as they would. When they were filled, he said unto his disciples, gather up the fragments that remain, that nothing be lost.*

As the men were connected to the instruction of Jesus, the provision of God flowed through them to their wives and children. Jesus was the source, and he chose to use the men as the resource.

The Ultimate Mark of Manhood Is Understanding That God Is the Source of Fulfillment.

2. A MAN'S RELATIONSHIP WITH HIS WIFE

I know that somebody is asking, "What about girlfriends?" Of course, it matters how a man treats all women; however, there is no divine covenant between a man and his girlfriend. A man's relationship to his wife is absolutely vital.

The Relationship That Truly Impacts or Impairs a Man's Future Is His Relationship with His Wife.

The Bible is very direct in this matter. It says, in 1 Peter 3:7: *Likewise, ye husbands, dwell with them according to knowledge, giving honour unto the wife, as unto the weaker vessel, and as being heirs together of the grace of life; that your prayers be not hindered.*

This is a powerful passage. It indicates that a wrong relationship to one's wife may very well prohibit a man's dreams.

It is very important that a man is mature enough to actually relate to a wife. If he treats her with honor, he invites the favor of God.

The way a man manages his relationship with the woman he is in covenant with, is the determining factor in how his plans come together. God takes a man's conduct and attitude with his wife very seriously.

The Bible explicitly instructs, in Proverbs 18:22: *Whoso findeth a wife findeth a good thing, and obtaineth favour of the Lord.*

A wife brings favor. A man must be conscious enough and secure enough within himself to recognize and receive a wife. When he is, he opens up the favor of God in his life. A wife comes with favor.

What Is a Wife?

Every woman is not a wife, yet all women have wife potential. However, all have not embraced the development process. A man must be capable of differentiating between those women who are conscious of their inner greatness and those who are not conscious. A woman must be aware of her inner greatness to manifest it. A wife is one who knows who she is and what she possesses.

Genesis 2:18 says: *And the Lord God said, It is not good that the man should be alone; I will make him an help meet for him.*

The first wife was defined by God as the man's "help." A wife is the man's help.

A Wife Is the Man's Soul Mate. She Is Ordained by God to Help Him to Manifest His Potential.

This means a few things. It means that the man must have something in place for a wife to assist with; and he must be man enough to embrace her gifts without feeling intimidated or belittled by her help. A wife cannot help a man who has no vision or is too insecure to accommodate her gifts.

A man who is doing nothing does not need a wife. A wife is only necessary for a man who has a clear purpose and vision. When a man only considers the sexual benefits of a wife, he is far too shallow.

A man who is struggling with insecurities and self-esteem issues is not a good candidate for a wife. A wife is a grown, capable and gifted woman, reserved for a comparable man. She's a queen paired with a king. It is tragic to place a wife in the care of a man-child. Don't be a man-child, brother. Be a king.

When a Man Recognizes His Wife's Purpose and Contribution, He Then Has the Perspective to Love Her Properly.

The Bible states, in Ephesians 5:25–29: *Husbands, love your wives, even as Christ also loved the church, and gave himself for it; That he might sanctify and cleanse it with the washing of water by the word, That he might present it to himself a glorious church, not having spot, or wrinkle, or any such thing; but that it should be holy and without blemish. So ought men to love their wives as their own bodies. He that loveth his wife loveth himself. For no man ever yet hated his own flesh; but nourisheth and cherisheth it, even as the Lord the church.*

This text reveals quite a bit, regarding the intangible qualities of a true husband's psychological and spiritual makeup. It suggests that he will sacrifice himself, help to improve his wife's condition, never do anything to harm his wife, and will cherish his wife as most precious.

It Takes a Grown and Selfless Man to Be a True Husband.

A major part of loving your wife, as a man, is in being patient and empathetic. Understanding your wife's emotional makeup, and her physical and psychological needs, are all a part of loving your wife effectively.

Every level of the relationship with your wife will demand a deeper dimension of understanding. To cherish her is to place such a value on her that you will protect her with all carefulness.

Being a Husband is More Than Being a Husband in the Bedroom. A Man Must Know His Wife Beyond the Physical. He Must Have a Fix on Her Soul.

There are many changes a woman goes through and many needs she will have that will require the wisdom of a husband to help her navigate. For instance, if you are blessed to grow to a certain age, you will come to a stage called "hurricane menopause." This is when she goes through hormonal changes that throw her emotions from one extreme to the other. Her body goes completely out of control and she doesn't even understand what's going on. She can't even explain what's happening because she does not know.

It would be very easy, for a grown boy, to jump ship during this season. The reality is, this is when she needs you to be the man like never before; in fact, you won't survive this season unless you are a full-grown man. You must pay attention and manage her skillfully and never emotionally, or harshly.

Manhood Is Patience.

Another season to be mindful of is immediately after childbirth. When a young woman's body has been ravaged by the reality of carrying another human being for months, and delivering the equivalent to a cantaloupe, it impacts her self-esteem. She does not feel attractive or desirable any longer, both of which are extremely important to a woman. The way she defines her femininity becomes confused. She may not articulate her feelings. It will require that you discern her heart and meet her need for esteem.

Your wife's self-esteem is your responsibility. Just like a father builds his daughter's self-esteem, a husband is responsible to keep his wife's esteem bank full. You cannot do this if you are oblivious to her deeper needs.

I find that a constant and intentional dialogue about life will keep a man supplied with clues concerning his wife's emotional condition. You must talk with your wife about more than bills, sex and children.

Developing the habit of observation will also prove to be extremely valuable. If you pay attention to her, you will detect what's going on with her without her having to say anything. That's your job.

Do not become angry and bitter with your wife so easily. There will be times when you will feel unfairly caught up in a tornado of emotion. Know that it is not about you. It is a signal that your woman needs you. Be there.

I remember a major blowout Lisa and I had. I must admit that I got angry and said some hurtful things. I was done! I didn't understand all of the emotions a woman sometimes goes through. I did not feel like I deserved the changes we were going through. I did something that I am completely ashamed of, even until this day: I communicated the idea that I was finished. In my mind, I was checking out emotionally. I was going to make her sorry for these emotions she was feeling.

I never will forget that she said to me, in the midst of all of this drama, "You are all I have." Wow! I was taking this personally when the entire time this was my wife crying out for support and help from her husband. What a fool I was! Don't be a fool.

The Word of God gives us a very direct order in Colossians 3:19, which says: *Husbands, love your wives, and be not bitter against them.*

3. A MAN'S RELATIONSHIP WITH HIS CHILDREN

It is sad that our concepts of fatherhood are as archaic as the Roman Colosseum's remains. We are in a new millennium and are still fathering as if we are from the Stone Age.

Most Men Believe That the Extent of Fathering Is to Put Food on the Table.

Think about how sad that is. If that is the extent of your responsibility to a living soul who is of your seed, you can be replaced by the U.S. Government. The U.S. Government can put food on the table. In fact, taxpayers are feeding millions of kids whose biological fathers don't even participate financially. How sad.

It's interesting how the man's relationships unfold. His relationship with God is the precursor for his relationship with his wife. His relationship with his wife is the foundation of his relationship with his children.

A Man's Relationship with His Children Starts with Their Mother.

The single greatest thing a man may do for his children is to love their mother. Before kids hear anything you may say, they are observing the interaction between you and the person they knew before they entered the world. They knew their mother from the womb. You cannot mistreat a child's mother and love the child properly.

For instance, it takes a very dumb man to argue and fight with a woman who is carrying his child. Granted, she may be a difficult and negative person; however, she is carrying your seed! Whatever energy you create or entertain is going beyond you and her; it is resting in the spirit of your child. A grown man learns to monitor the moment and behave accordingly.

The wisdom of Solomon says, in Proverbs 20:3: *It is an honour for a man to cease from strife: but every fool will be meddling.*

Kings function with discretion. Mothers are the incubators of the future generations. Whatever a man puts into his woman will infect his children.

A Man Must Be Present in His Children's Lives.

Too many times, as fathers, we allow our children to drift too long before we engage with them. It's usually when there is a crisis that we are responding to, and we want to fly in to save the day. Too often the crisis is the consequence of our emotional absence. Our children have a negative reaction to our absence. They may be smiling and excelling, but something is breaking inside them as a result of our apparent disregard.

Fathers Provide an Example of Manhood for Their Sons and They Infuse Self-Esteem into Their Daughters. The Princess Needs the King's Voice; the Prince Needs the King's Praise.

There's a wisdom found in Psalms 127:3–5, which says: *Lo, children are an heritage of the Lord: and the fruit of the womb is his reward. As arrows are in the hand of a mighty man; so are children of the youth. Happy is the man that hath his quiver full of them: they shall not be ashamed, but they shall speak with the enemies in the gate.*

A quiver holds the arrows of the archer; it rests alongside the archer. It's closest to his hand. A good father keeps his children close by. He keeps his hand on them. He's ever-present.

I once had a parental philosophy that said "grown and gone." One day, my adult children made me understand how much they still needed me. I actually believed that I was through. Not so. Your children will always require your presence.

> Never Promise to Be There and
> Not Show Up Without a Real Explanation.
> It Breeds Disrespect and Contempt.

Children have no concept of money or responsibility. They can't place a value on tuition, mortgage payments or the need to be at a job. They are kids. They don't understand why these things may take up your time and perceive this as a rejection of them. This will slowly breed low self-esteem.

When you legitimately cannot be present, you should sit them down and explain why. You should make a big deal out of the occasion you have missed and rush to hear a detailed explanation of everything that happened. Your interest will disrupt the concept of rejection. The main thing is to show up, more times than not.

> We Must Respect Our Kids.

As men, we are usually big on respect. We demand to be respected by women, in our jobs and with our friends, and we definitely demand respect from our children. The issue is this: respect is not really something we should demand; we should command it. Respect should be the consequence of your character, not the product of aggression.

> When You Command Respect,
> You Never Have to Demand It.

When it comes to our kids, few of us ever think that we owe them as much respect as we are demanding from them.

The Apostle Paul makes it plain in his letter to the church at Ephesus. It says, in Ephesians 6:4: *And, ye fathers, provoke not your children to wrath: but bring them up in the nurture and admonition of the Lord.*

We cannot terrorize our kids and expect them to grow into well-adjusted adults who know how to carry themselves in the world.

Most Adults Are Struggling to Recover from Their Childhood.

The disrespect we force upon our kids may turn into passivity, in adulthood. They may become voiceless doormats for society. On the flip side, they may become aggressive and behave like terrorists to prove themselves powerful. Disrespectful parenting does not usually end well.

We disrespect our kids by chastising them without instruction. You can't just scream at a kid and exact stiff punishment or worse without giving the child an understanding of why you're doing it. They need to know what they've done wrong.

It's Disrespectful to Chastise a Kid You Never Talk to or Lovingly Instruct.

It is disrespectful to treat a teenaged kid as though they are ten. It is not wise to fail to understand that you must adjust your parenting according to the child's age. To parent a kid out of season will breed rebellion, every time. Even if they are behaving like a younger child, it will require wisdom on your part to break through and to help them to evolve.

It is disrespectful to fly off the handle without getting the kid's position. Many times, we attack our kids on somebody else's word, before we've allowed our children to share their side of the story. This is not wise. This establishes a culture of distrust for you. You become the enemy. They may never trust you with their secrets in life. Every move we make has the potential to leave a wound in the hearts of our kids. The sad reality is that most of the time it is totally unintentional.

> Many Father Wounds (Emotional Wounds, in Children, Caused by Fathers) Are Unintentional.

4. A MAN'S RELATIONSHIP WITH SPIRITUAL AUTHORITY

A man needs spiritual accountability in his life. In my opinion, those that function as spiritual fathers and mentors are vital to the man's development. Natural fathers are sometimes scarce or not present at all, when a man comes of age. In some cases, he's not the best example. While a man could not control the presence of his natural father, he has the wonderful ability to seek a worthy spiritual guide on his journey to manhood. Never misconstrue or misinterpret the concept of a spiritual father.

> A Spiritual Father Is a Godly Man Who Serves as an Example and Guide for a Younger Man's Future. He Is One Whom the Younger Man Senses in His Spirit to Be the Model of Godliness and Manhood.

Society creates this toxic tension between men and spiritual leaders. In fact, sometimes poor examples of leaders work to destroy the trust men should have in them. It's no secret that we have perverts, pedophiles and others who are nothing short of pimps, sitting in high places in religion.

On the other hand, God has a system where he will orchestrate the connection between every man and a man of good report. Don't allow the publicized degenerates to destroy your faith in all spiritual leaders. Judge every man based on his own character.

The writer of Hebrews gives us a major life principle. Hebrews 6:12 says: *That ye be not slothful, but followers of them who through faith and patience inherit the promises.*

We all need someone to follow. Every man needs an example. The day we become cynical and don't want to be open to the guidance of another man is the day we limit ourselves.

A Man Should Be Led to Lead. It's Not Who You're Over, It's Who You're Under.

In 1 Corinthians 11:1–3, it states: *Be ye followers of me, even as I also am of Christ. Now I praise you, brethren, that ye remember me in all things, and keep the ordinances, as I delivered them to you. But I would have you know, that the head of every man is Christ; and the head of the woman is the man; and the head of Christ is God.*

The Apostle Paul admonishes the Corinthian Church to follow him as he follows Christ. Manhood is about following. Great leaders are great followers.

A Man Needs Spiritual Accountability to Help Him to See Himself at Times.

One of the more practical aspects in the value of spiritual authority that is present in a man's life is the idea of having someone to hold the man accountable. Who corrects a grown man when he is off base? In many cases it takes a man to challenge a man. It can't be any man to challenge a king; that might be a fight. It will require a man who has earned an honorable position in the man's life. He will have to be one who is respected and highly esteemed.

There's a record of a spiritual father addressing the transgressions of King David. It required a special voice to correct King David. David didn't play by the rules. David was known for killing people who offended him. There was one prophet by the name of Nathan who was in David's life. He was the man whom David viewed as his spiritual authority.

David had fallen off the wagon. He committed adultery, got another man's wife pregnant, had the man killed and married the man's wife. Nobody checked David's morality on this issue, but Nathan held him accountable.

In 2 Samuel 12:7, it says: *And Nathan said to David, Thou art the man. Thus saith the Lord God of Israel, I anointed thee king over Israel, and I delivered thee out of the hand of Saul.*

Nathan made David aware that his behavior displeased God. When Nathan was finished, David ran to God and repented.

Every Man Needs a Relationship with a Strong Man Who Will Bring Out the Best in Him.

CHAPTER 6

THE HARMONY OF KINGS AND QUEENS
How Kings and Queens Find Each Other and Function in Sync

There's an interesting dynamic between kings and queens. There's an unconditioned harmony between the king-conscious man and the queen-conscious woman. It's not a chemistry that is fabricated or based on mind-numbing lust. It is a harmony that can only be described as God-ordained. It is the connection Adam and Eve had. When Adam first laid eyes on Eve, he said, "This is bone of my bones and flesh of my flesh." It was a witness on the spiritual level.

When Kingology Meets Queenology, the Chemistry Is Amazing.

There's a lot to be said for a man and woman who are on the same emotional, intellectual and spiritual frequency. When a king meets his queen, the connection is electric.

Many women will possess an attractiveness and passion, but there's a deeper level called purpose. When a king meets a queen, he senses his future in that woman. He senses purpose. She is, then, deemed critical to his destiny.

Going back to Adam and Eve, when the Bible called Eve a *help meet* it referred to her as being suitable for Adam. It meant that she had everything Adam needed. There are not a lot of women who will possess everything you need. When you find that one, you must take action.

Again, it is stated, in Genesis 2:18: *And the Lord God said, It is not good that the man should be alone; I will make him an help meet for him.*

When God created Adam's queen, he made her suitable for him. It was not a relationship that had to be forced. Eve had everything Adam needed. She was suitable physically, mentally and spiritually. She was fitting for his present and his future.

A King Needs a Queen Who Meets All of His Needs in One Woman.

The woman in Proverbs 31 was this sort of wife to her husband.

Proverbs 31:10-12 says: *Who can find a virtuous woman? for her price is far above rubies. The heart of her husband doth safely trust in her, so that he shall have no need of spoil. She will do him good and not evil all the days of her life.*

Notice how the virtuous woman did her husband good, and he had no need of spoil. He had no excuse. He had no justifiable reason for messing up. It takes a certain caliber of woman to fit a king. A queen covers all of the bases in her man's life. She leaves nothing for another woman to have. She's a queen and rules her kingdom, of which the king is the center.

A King Must Have a Queen.

Anything less than a queen-conscious woman becomes a frustration for the king. He soon discovers that it is futile to have settled for a woman who has an inferior perspective. A woman who works on her bustline, and never her bottom line, is irritating. A woman who has phenomenal potential and no drive to realize it is a disappointment to a king. He thrives on maximizing potential. His woman must share that philosophy. A queen boils down to the equivalent of a king in female form. They think and move the same.

One of the great deceptions of kings is to waste too much time with women who only awaken you on levels that are less important and have nothing to do with your destiny. Many men waste valuable time on dating women who clearly cannot play a role in their present or future kingdom.

Sex and Cuteness Don't Create Legacy.

FACTS ABOUT THE HARMONY BETWEEN A KING AND HIS QUEEN

1. ONLY THE TWO CAN SATISFY EACH OTHER

A king cannot be content with less than a queen; and a queen cannot be satisfied with less than a king. Many men extend temporary relationships and attempt to make something permanent of them. Some women are only a date. Some are just friends. It is what it is: kings need queens. Only a queen can truly satisfy a king.

What Is a King?

A king is a man who is in full awareness of his power, his purpose and his mission. He understands that he lives to protect and empower everything in his care and to cause things to flourish.

What Is a Queen?

A queen is a woman who understands her role in life. She is completely conscious of who she is, apart from what she's gone through. She walks with a certainty and confidence. Nobody can do what she's been anointed to do.

These two are never replaceable. A king will always need his queen. He may settle for less, but he will never be fulfilled without his queen. He may never manifest his greatest potential without his queen.

The Queen Is Essential to the Complete Manifestation of the King.

The Word of God defines what Eve's name meant, in Genesis 3:20: *And Adam called his wife's name Eve; because she was **the mother of all living**.*

The first woman's name meant "mother of all living." The queen is essential because she is the one to give life to everything the man sees or possesses. Where there's no queen, there's only potential. No birthing.

Think of how frustrating it would be to know that you have Michael Jordan, Hall-of-Fame-type NBA talent, but you only rise as high as the D league. This is a great depiction of how a man's life may be stymied by the failure to add the right woman to his process. The queen causes everything in you to come forth. Just like a woman takes a man's seed and reproduces his children, she has the same ability to bring life to everything in the man's heart. Of course, we are talking about the right woman.

The Dominion God Ordered Is Only Activated When Kings and Queens Live in Covenant.

Remember what Genesis 1:28 says: *And God blessed them, and God said unto them, Be fruitful, and multiply, and replenish the earth, and subdue it: and have dominion over the fish of the sea, and over the fowl of the air, and over every living thing that moveth upon the earth.*

This is the textual proof that dominion was always designed to be a cooperative grace, shared between man and woman. *This is not to say that one cannot dominate apart from marriage.* Jesus was not married. It is to say that one must embrace life from the perspective of cooperation.

Even if a man never has a mind to marry, he must recognize the contribution of the women in his life. His mother, sisters, friends, coworkers and employees will all have a significant grace to contribute to his rise.

God Has Given Women a Grace to Pull Things Together and to Materialize What's in a Man's Heart.

God pronounced dominion onto "them." There's something supernatural that transpires when a king recognizes his queen and solidifies the covenant relationship before God.

Please do not allow a perverted society that is speedily moving further away from God's principles and biblical values to convince you to ignore the covenant of marriage.

When a Man Finds the Right Woman, He Hinders Himself If He Doesn't Seal It in Marriage.

I am aware that this is a different day and time. Marriage is no longer a pre-requisite. We create entire families without any official covenant. Gone are the days of marriage and commitment. If that is your position, you have a right to be wrong. You can laugh right here; it wasn't a misprint. The point is, God still blesses marriage and strong men thrive on commitments and covenants.

The Favor You Need Upon Your Life Is Waiting in Your Wife.

Of course, a man can succeed without a wife; men do it all of the time. Adam did it before Eve was created. However, there's something extraordinary that happens when a man can recognize a woman as his wife and honor her in the covenant of marriage. God brings that man to a new dimension.

Proverbs 18:22 says: *Whoso findeth a wife findeth a good thing, and obtaineth favour of the Lord.*

The idea that the man is conscious enough to recognize a wife indicates that this is a grown man; he knows what he needs and takes care of business to secure it. Grown men are searching for a wife.

What's the Difference Between a Man Looking for Sex Versus a Man Searching for a Wife?

When we look at the contrast between a man who only sees the sexuality of a woman and never looks for the substance of a wife, on the one hand, and the man who seeks a wife, on the other, we see a stark difference in the results and consequences.

The Bible records the fate of a man who is driven by the woman's sexuality alone. This is found in Proverbs 6:26, which says: *For by means of a whorish woman a man is brought to a piece of bread: and the adulteress will hunt for the precious life.*

The man described in this text is driven by lust and is just looking for sex; he loses everything! How many times have we seen this? A man captivated by the curves of an illicit woman is lured into her curse. He probably looked over many great wives, to land on a trick.

The first guy, in Proverbs 18:22, is looking for something deeper than the sexual. He recognizes wife material. He recognizes a wife because a wife is what he is looking for. The Bible says that favor (blessing) flooded his life.

It takes a true queen to satisfy a king's many needs. Anything less is a waste. When a man detects that a woman has what he's looking for, he makes a decision.

Sometimes, as men, we, for whatever reason, play games with the woman we know is destined to be our queen. In a lot of cases we lose that woman to another, more decisive man. How tragic it is to see a woman you know was perfect for you on the arm of another man.

That almost happened to me; in fact, it did happen to me. I was trying to break up with Lisa and she immediately accepted my wishes. I was completely blown away. I had never had a woman accept my breakup so readily.

A few months later, I heard that she had met another guy. He was a professional baseball player. I tried to play it off, but I was tormented. I knew this woman and I were meant to be together. At that point, pride intervened, and I was delirious with jealousy. Some of you know what I'm talking about.

To make a long story short, I called her after nearly a year and articulated my love, and my desire for a lifelong commitment. To my surprise, she accepted and broke it off with the other guy. I almost missed the woman who was perfect for my life and future. I almost missed my queen because of insecurity and indecision.

2. THE TWO MUST DISCERN EACH OTHER

Kings and queens do not announce themselves, or project themselves. Only those qualified to know them will see them. Sometimes kings don't look like kings and queens don't look like queens. David was anointed king before he ever looked like it. He was a skinny little shepherd boy, and yet he was King of Israel. Esther was a simple little girl who was raised by a cousin. She did not look like a queen.

It Takes a King's Perception to Discern a Queen.

Many women struggle because they know their own worth and cannot figure out why there are not more men in pursuit of them. The answer, though it does little to satisfy the woman's feelings, is that it takes a king to know a queen. Most men are not yet king-conscious, and therefore view life from the very low frequency of visual stimulation and sexual gratification. Most men are not yet equipped to look deeper. Queens possess depth.

Rest and Security Are the Fruit of the Synergy Between Kings and Queens.

There are some consistent and distinct things that the king and queen produce in each other's lives.

If we return to Genesis and look at Adam and Eve, we can see yet another demonstration of the dynamics of the relationship, when kings and queens are in harmony.

The Word of God says, in Genesis 2:21–23: *And the Lord God caused a deep sleep to fall upon Adam, and he slept: and he took one of his ribs, and closed up the flesh instead thereof; And the rib, which the Lord God had taken from man, made he a woman, and brought her unto the man. And Adam said, This is now bone of my bones, and flesh of my flesh: she shall be called Woman, because she was taken out of Man.*

This was the first time we see Adam resting. This is interesting and revealing at the same time. While God was creating Adam's queen, Adam rested. I believe that there is an argument for a subliminal message being communicated to the male psyche here.

A Man Discerns His Queen by the Woman Who Creates a Space for His Mind, Body and Spirit to Rest.

Once again, we return to the virtuous woman and her husband. It states, in Proverbs 31:11–12: *The heart of her husband doth safely trust in her, so that he shall have no need of spoil. She will do him good and not evil all the days of her life.*

She created a space and place for her husband to rest. His home and his wife were his resting place. A man discerns his queen by the woman who offers him rest.

When we look at Eve, in the creation, she was created from within Adam. She was made from his rib, a place of tenderness and security. A woman's king will always love her as his own flesh. He will treat her as though his very life depends on her safety and satisfaction.

A Woman Discerns Her Husband by the Man Who Makes Her Feel Safe and Cared For.

The Apostle Paul teaches this in Ephesians 5:28–30: *So ought men to love their wives as their own bodies.*

He that loveth his wife loveth himself. For no man ever yet hated his own flesh; but nourisheth and cherisheth it, even as the Lord the church.

This is a direct instruction for a man to love, protect and cherish his wife like Jesus does the church. A woman needs this from her king.

When a Woman Feels Safe in Every Way, She Will Be Free to Submit.

How few men today actually have been trained to even consider these matters, when it comes to their women. We are so insensitive to a woman's real needs that we function almost like new age cavemen.

How many times have you provided everything but a true sense of security? Being willing and able to physically fight for your woman is honorable; however, you have the responsibility to assure that her heart feels safe.

Don't Be a Man Who Protects His Woman's Body Only to Break Her Soul.

When the king and the queen are developed enough to actually see each other, understand each other and serve each other, the outcome is an amazing connection rooted in dominion. Nothing can stop them. They become invincible.

3. THE TWO NEVER COMPETE; THEY ONLY COMPLEMENT EACH OTHER

To observe the interaction between a true king and queen is like watching a brilliant ballroom dance routine; the maneuvers are intricate and complex, yet there is a fluid grace and synergy to them that is mesmerizing. They never seem to run into each other or interfere with the other's space. They are closer to each other than anyone else in the world and yet they synchronize.

The kingdom requires a multifaceted approach. It's no kingdom if only one person may run it. This requires the two to have a mature level of respect and comfort with each other.

The king is not threatened by the queen's brilliance and drive, nor is the queen seeking to supplant the king's position. They both coexist for the advancement of one kingdom.

Recently, Lisa and I have been blessed to develop a cherished friendship with Dr. Ira Hilliard and Dr. Bridgett Hilliard. If you don't know these people, you should get to know them. They are generals who have literally impacted the world for Jesus Christ.

In spending time with them I have observed a few things: they are both equally strong leaders, and they both have specific aspects of expertise in the ministry empire they have built. I've also observed that he has no problem with allowing her to take the lead in her areas of expertise. She always works to glorify Jesus and she makes her king look good in the process. He does the same for her. It is a beautiful synchronization of two independent gifts flowing together for a common goal. Never is there intimidation or competition; they are forever complementing each other, and they continue to climb higher.

The Bible gives us a powerful principle of unity and oneness. When people—especially a king and his queen—are on the same page, without the drama, miracles happen.

In Genesis 11:6, it states: *And the Lord said, Behold, the people is one, and they have all one language; and this they begin to do: and now nothing will be restrained from them, which they have imagined to do.*

This scripture is not specifically about unity in a relationship. This is a depiction of the unity within a nation, and the unlimited power it produced for all involved. Because the people were undivided and totally unified without any contention, even God recognized that nothing would be impossible for them.

How much more of a massive impact would the unity of a king and queen produce, when there is no competition?

4. KINGS AND QUEENS HAVE GROWTH CAPACITY

There's nothing more emotionally draining than to be saddled with a relationship that has exhausted its growth potential. To be joined to a person who is not suitable is miserable.

The most beautiful impact of the harmony between kings and queens is that there is no limit to where they can go, or what they can produce. There are no limits on their relationship. It's like living in a building with no roof, or a room with no ceiling. They can go as far as they can imagine going.

When a King Identifies and Solidifies His Covenant with His Queen, His Capacity Is Multiplied.

Again, we return to the book of Genesis for enlightenment. In Genesis 1:27–28, once again it says: *So, God created man in his own image, in the image of God created he him; male and female created he them. And God blessed them, and God said unto them, Be fruitful, and multiply, and replenish the earth, and subdue it: and have dominion over the fish of the sea, and over the fowl of the air, and over every living thing that moveth upon the earth.*

What we see here are what I call the tenets of dominion. A tenet is a principle or philosophy. God established the marriage between Adam and Eve. God established the concept of dominion and established Adam and Eve as the co-beneficiaries of His will.

The first thing God assigns to dominion is fruitfulness. When the two are flowing together they are fruitful. In other words, their union causes an increase in resources. Kings and queens always function from a place of abundance. The second aspect of dominion is multiplication. The resources they accumulate are always compounding. They are shifting dimensions when others are struggling to get to the next level. The third concept of dominion is the capacity to replenish. Kings and queens always restore what they've taken or used. They are assets to their communities. The final principle of dominion is to subdue. Kings and queens always take control of their environment. They always possess territory. To subdue territory, in this sense, means that they will prosper and succeed in any environment. They will naturally rise to the top in any situation they are in.

There Are No Limits When a King Has a Queen He Harmonizes with.

CHAPTER 7

KINGS AND COINS
A King's Respect for Money

In this chapter we are discussing the man and money. I chose to title it "Kings and Coins," because it just flowed so well phonetically. It sounds good, but we are talking about men and money.

The man's relationship to money is a reflection of his character and maturity. Most of the world's problems are due to men who have an ungodly and disrespectful relationship to money. Wars are started because of money. Policies that hurt defenseless people are promoted and approved because of money.

> Money, Itself, Is Not Evil; The Man's Love and Obsession for It Is Evil.

Let's glean some wisdom from the scriptures. In 1 Timothy 6:9–10, it says: *But they that will be rich fall into temptation and a snare, and into many foolish and hurtful lusts, which drown men in destruction and perdition. For the love of money is the root of all evil: which while some coveted after, they have erred from the faith, and pierced themselves through with many sorrows.*

We may always discern a man who has not had much of a relationship with money, at least not a healthy relationship. He always believes that money is the source of happiness. He defines himself by his bank account and he is obsessed with making money. Consequently, he makes a living without ever building a life.

Kings understand the purpose of money and they never allow themselves to be lost in society's false idea that money may replace the vital aspects of life. Money will never replace God. Money cannot purchase peace.

Money cannot replace relationships. Money is important, but money is not supreme.

Money Has a Purpose in a Man's Life. A King Keeps the Coins in Context.

Money is the servant of the man, while the man is the servant of God. Kings do not allow money to possess their hearts and souls. Kings use money, while never allowing the money to use them.

Jesus put it this way, in Matthew 6:24: *No man can serve two masters; for either he will hate the one and love the other, or he will be devoted to the one and despise the other. You cannot serve God and mammon [money, possessions, fame, status, or whatever is valued more than the Lord].*

This text speaks of a person who has an inappropriate relationship to money. Any man who functions as such will ultimately find himself in an immoral abyss; he'll be unhappy and unfulfilled.

A king-conscious man is a man who has overcome the excitement of having means, and the thrill of new things. He does not need pseudo forms of power, because he is powerful. Kings know the true purpose and potential of money and have no desire for showing off. They have no stomach for the unnecessary accumulation of, material things.

When we look at our brothers today, we see a parade of grown boys with big toys. We see massive amounts of waste that could be used to do much good in society. We witness men with low self-esteem attempting to purchase confidence. Don't be that guy. He's viewed as the equivalent of a clown in certain realms of society. Don't be a clown. Be a king.

The Word of God describes a wasteful man in some less-than-flattering terms. It states, in Proverbs 21:20: *There is treasure to be desired and oil in the dwelling of the wise; but a foolish man spendeth it up.*

A man must develop a mature and balanced relationship with money. For every man, he may get a scan of his own soul by the management of his money.

A man's spirituality, priorities and maturity are all on display when he looks at his bank statements. A man's heart is reflected in his financial habits and choices. A man's credit score may very well be an indication of his emotional maturity. Many of the financial difficulties I experienced as a young man were the product of childish priorities. As my heart matured my financial choices followed.

The Bible says, in Matthew 6:21: *For where your treasure is, there will your heart be also.*

When You Follow the Money, You Eventually Arrive at Your Heart.

A man may get an X-ray of his heart, when he observes his financial life. Men cannot afford to be financially reckless or childish. Money is not a toy; it is a tool. It can build or kill, depending on whose hands it is in. A man must never be found to be irresponsible with financial resources.

THERE ARE TWO MAIN REASONS A MAN MUST MANAGE MONEY

1. A MAN IS THE DEFENDER OF THE FAMILY

The Bible says in Ecclesiastes 7:12 says: *For wisdom is a defence, and money is a defence.* A conscious man understands money as a means to defend himself and his family. There are many predicaments that will simply require having enough money. A child's education, a parent's health care, and a wife's need for more space are all examples of things that a man can only answer when he has resources. Nothing gives a husband and father greater pride than being able to meet the financial challenges of the family. Nothing breaks his spirit like having no answer for the serious needs of his family. Imagine what it must feel like to be helpless in the face of crisis, when you actually had the resources, but you squandered them.

There's Nothing Worse Than Not Having Enough, When You Once Had More Than Enough.

The Word of God says, in 1 Timothy 5:8, in the Amplified version: *If anyone fails to provide for his relatives, and especially for those of his own family, he has disowned the faith [by failing to accompany it with fruits] and is worse than an unbeliever [who performs his obligation in these matters].*

One of the basic fruits of manhood is a man striving to provide for his own. If there is no desire to provide and protect, we have missed the fundamental psychology of manhood.

2. A MAN IS THE VISIONARY OF THE FAMILY

A mature man sees money as the future in tangible form. Money may be a forecast of a preferred future. It is a man's role to see where the family can go and to chart a path to get there. One of the most vital components of a vision is to determine where the provision may come from.

When a man handles money, he views it as the down payment on a greater tomorrow for his children and grandchildren.

Proverbs 13:22 says: *A good man leaveth an inheritance to his children's children.*

A King Is Always Securing the Future of His Kingdom.

There is nothing a man may do, after he has died. However, if he has managed money properly, his impact may touch the generations to come.

The Bible also states, in Ecclesiastes 10:19: *A feast is made for laughter, and wine maketh merry: but money answereth all things.*

Money will provide answers for a man's grandchildren. On this note, every responsible man must apply himself to understanding the language of trusts versus wills, insurance and real estate versus trading and investments. Money has language.

The Success of a Man Is Determined by the Power of His Successors.

THE MIND-SET OF A GROWN MAN AND MONEY

It was a fascinating experience to witness my own financial evolution as a man. When I was a kid, I viewed money as a means to secure an image or to purchase self-gratification. As I grew in my mind-set, my philosophy about the attainment of money and the disbursement of it shifted drastically. A grown man thinks differently about money.

1. HE HAS A MIND TO WORK FOR IT

For a king-conscious man, it is not only important to have money; it is equally important to earn it. Kings do not steal. Kings do not leach off their community. Kings do not rob.

Kings Earn Their Money.

In 2 Thessalonians 3:10, it says: *For even when we were with you, this we commanded you, that if any would not work, neither should he eat.*

My father and mentor, Robert Blakes, Sr., taught my brother and I to work for our money. He was a very successful man, but he never allowed us to feel entitled. He gave us very little of what we wanted. He provided everything we needed and taught us to work hard for the rest. It was one of the greatest manhood drills he could have ever enforced.

I remember an occasion when my mother purchased a pair of shoes for me that cost $60. I was about thirteen years of age. My father thought it was too much. He made me take the shoes back and get a cheaper pair of shoes. His actual words were: "A man who wears $60 shoes should have a paycheck to match." I was fuming then, but I understand now.

2. HE HAS A MIND TO PAY HIS BILLS

A real man will never willingly be in a position where he owes anyone anything. Men pay their bills. Real men have good reputations for being true to their word. Nothing reflects a man's character like his debt philosophy. A real man does not sleep well when he owes a debt. Proverbs 22:1 says: *A good name is rather to be chosen than great riches, and loving favour rather than silver and gold.*

A Man's Credit Score Is Largely a Reflection of His Financial Reputation.

The Bible provides us with a very pragmatic rule for managing debt. It is found in Proverbs 3:27–28, and it states, in the Amplified version: *Withhold not good from those to whom it is due [its rightful owners], when it is in the power of your hand to do it. Do not say to your neighbor, Go, and come again; and tomorrow I will give it—when you have it with you.*

Kings pay their debts as soon as they have the means. Never procrastinate to pay your bills. Pay your bills on time. Never use 100% of your credit limit unless it's an emergency. Ideally, keep it beneath 10%–20% of your limit. Don't allow stores or institutions to run your credit too often; it negatively impacts your credit score. These are just a few things that most of us are never taught, and we suffer for it. I'm no financial consultant, but we all must be basic students of how money, debt and credit work. It's important.

3. HE HAS A MIND TO SAVE MONEY

This point goes back to the concept of men being the protectors of the family. A big part of defending the family lies in saving money for emergencies. Men are responsible for meeting sudden needs and challenges with means. It is a pitiful man who is comfortable being broke and powerless to aid his family in the face of need.

Kings Never Spend It All.

The wisdom of the Holy Scripture says, in Proverbs 6:6–8: *Go to the ant, thou sluggard; consider her ways, and be wise: Which having no guide, overseer, or ruler, Provideth her meat in the summer, and gathereth her food in the harvest.*

The ant has a concern and strategy to address the demands of the lean seasons. Seasons are repetitive. We experience times of plenty and times of scarcity. We must use the plentiful times to provide for the scarce seasons.

A true king has foresight. He makes preparation for the possibilities that common men never consider. I remember my father saving cans filled with coins. When we had difficult days, my father would bring those coins to the bank and they would pull us through. I have the same habit today. I never spend it all. As the foundation of my family I always make certain that there is something somewhere to pull from.

As a pastor, I even put money aside in the event my church may need help in some area. On more than one occasion I have dipped into our personal resources to assist my ministry financially.

Kings Are Always Prepared to Respond.

You won't be able to do it if you have all of your resources sitting in a garage or a closet. Nobody loves nice cars and fine clothing more than I do, but there are other things that are a necessity. Never spend it all.

It's uncanny how the resources a man puts aside always seem to be exactly what's needed. There's no greater feeling than having been the one to have been responsible enough to provide for those most important in our lives.

SEVEN THINGS THAT DESTROY A MAN FINANCIALLY

1. WOMANIZING

When a man fails to overcome the temptations of lust and infidelity, he will have to pay a great price. He pays a spiritual price. He pays a social price. It costs him emotionally, and it will always hit his economic reality.

It Costs a Great Deal to Maintain an Illicit Lifestyle.

When a man is a cheater, he has to pay to keep the "woman on the side" happy. If not, she may talk to others, or post something about him on social media. If you're a single "player," it will drain you to pay for all of those dinners and clubs, not to mention alcohol and hotel rooms.

2. INDECISION

A man who cannot or will not make a decision will always pay a tremendous price. Many blessings and opportunities are time-sensitive. A man who flounders and procrastinates is easy prey for misfortune.

Some of the most regretful seasons of my life go back to times when I was paralyzed by insecurity and self-doubt. I just couldn't make a decision and I missed the opportune time to act. I eventually took action, but it did not accomplish what it could have, if I had acted earlier.

> Inaction Is the Forerunner of Failure.

James 1:8 says: *A double minded man is unstable in all his ways.*

Instability is always associated with a person who will not make a decision. It is an especially miserable position to be in when one is following a person who never decides anything. What must a wife and kids feel like following a man who never chooses? I imagine it must feel like being a passenger in a vehicle with a driver who is moving at full speed into a ditch and everyone else is doomed to observe the destruction of all.

3. GAMBLING

The culture promotes and supports the idea of gambling as a legitimate means of earning. I will not use this occasion to attempt to prove gambling to be a sin, or not. I will say this:

> A King Builds His Empire on Sound Decisions and Never on Chance.

Ecclesiastes 5:10 says, in the New American Standard Bible version: *He who loves money will not be satisfied with money, nor he who loves abundance with its income. This too is vanity.*

A man who is given to gambling quite often never gets enough and does not possess the discipline to stop. Gambling is associated with greed. Greed frequently ends in need. The Bible encourages us to simply exercise good stewardship of the things we possess. Good stewardship leads to increase.

I have never been a gambler. I would much rather use my money judiciously and take the long-term approach. Money that comes quickly often leaves just as fast.

4. LAZINESS IN BUSINESS

A man is always compromised when he does not have the discipline to apply himself to matters of business. If a man takes care of business, his business will take care of him. It will always show if a man fails to attend to his business. The daily acts of being on time, being consistently productive in whatever you put your hands to and being diligent are aspects of a man taking care of business.

So many feel as though they are entitled to success because they are gifted. We quote the scripture, which says, "A man's gift will make room for him." Making room versus owning the opportunity are two different things. So many men do not possess a corresponding work ethic to match their gifts. Every gift should have a business plan, and a business plan must have a businessman to work it.

Proverbs 22:29 says: *Seest thou a man diligent in his business? he shall stand before kings; he shall not stand before mean men.*

When you take care of your business and are enthusiastic, energetic and consistent you will have a never-ending parade of opportunities. A lazy man will have to beg for a break.

Opportunity Doesn't Knock for a Lazy Dude.

This is not a world for a lazy man. It takes energy and diligence to be a husband, father, provider, protector, leader and adviser, and to wear a million other hats. A man does not have the time to be lazy; too many people are depending on him. There are too many opportunities waiting on him. Wake up, brother!

5. OVERINDULGENCE IN RELAXATION

Kings do not focus on relaxation. Kings are consumed with advancement. Common men dream of vacations and leisure. Kings dream of opportunities and empires. Kings are constantly building.

Proverbs 6:9–11 states: *How long wilt thou sleep, O sluggard? when wilt thou arise out of thy sleep? Yet a little sleep, a little slumber, a little folding of the hands to sleep: So shall thy poverty come as one that travelleth, and thy want as an armed man.*

A lazy, lethargic man will never maintain the discipline to keep up with the need to earn and multiply resources. Lazy men will always end in want.

6. FLESHLY PASSIONS

A man who gives himself to wine, women and partying usually discovers himself surrounded by ruins. Stewardship demands the disciplining of a man's passions.

Proverbs 23:20–21 says: *Be not among winebibbers; among riotous eaters of flesh: For the drunkard and the glutton shall come to poverty: and drowsiness shall clothe a man with rags.*

7. GET-RICH-QUICK SCHEMES

The final issue I will address is that of the "get-rich-quick" scheme. As men, we are sometimes lured into the idea of quick wealth. This is rarely a reality. Most wealth will be the consequence of strategy, discipline and patience. A get-rich-quick scheme is really an oxymoron. One does not get rich quick; rather, one gets depleted quickly.

Proverbs 28:22 puts it this way: *He that hasteth to be rich hath an evil eye, and considereth not that poverty shall come upon him.*

As men, we must possess the same seriousness about money as a king feels for the financial health of his empire. Manhood does not afford us the luxury of irresponsibility. Too much is riding on our financial success.

CHAPTER 8

KINGS REGULATE THEIR EMOTIONS
Kings Maintain Control of Their Internal Stability

It is a bit different to discuss men and emotions in the same context. I come from an era where men were emotionally callous and unavailable. Men did not acknowledge pain or feelings. It was "gay" to be in touch with feelings. We were taught to just keep it in. Of course, there were many heart-attack victims from my era, for obvious reasons. Emotions are like pressure; they must have an outlet.

> My Generation Didn't Only Keep Our Issues In; We Also Kept Everybody Else Out.

Emotional intelligence is necessary for the health of the man, but it is crucial for the well-being of those he is responsible for. Any man who is incapable of acknowledging and processing his own emotions will always make for a toxic relationship. For you to be emotionally undisciplined, unavailable and ignorant makes you a problem to be close to. A man is challenged to provide his family with the tenderness they will need from their leader and if he cannot process his own emotions, he is nearly impossible for anyone to truly get to know.

Sometimes a man's wife does not really know him. The woman who shares marital vows with him and bears his children may not have a clue as to who he really is. The children, who have his genetics, share his features and carry his name, may not have the slightest understanding of who he is beneath the surface.

As a child, I spent a great deal of time with my mother's father, Mr. George Raymond, Sr. He was a family man who read the newspaper and was angry most of the time. This is the extent of what I know about my grandfather.

I loved him, but I never got to know him. He never got to know me. I spent about sixteen years of my life with him, before he died, and all I can tell you is that he was a family man, he was angry, and he read the newspaper.

It's impossible to know a man who is emotionally unavailable. As a father, husband, brother or son, you do not want your legacy to be that your family loved you but did not know you.

It Does Not Diminish Your Manhood to
Be Emotionally Authentic.

A complete opposite example of a man and his emotional availability would be my father. My dad was a stern "man's man," but at the same time, he was vulnerable and open to be explored. Dad would tell us of his most hurtful moments in life. He would talk about how certain things in his life made him feel. His emotional availability gave us a glimpse into his humanity. He wasn't so devoted to his machismo persona that he didn't connect his heart and soul to his family's understanding of him as a man. His willingness to be vulnerable gave us a perspective of him similar to that of Superman/Clark Kent. When a man can show both sides, he creates a balanced understanding of manhood for his sons and daughters.

Masculinity Must Always Be Balanced with Humanity to Maintain a Sense of Safety.

It's much easier for the world to trust a man who is in touch with his emotions than it is a man who appears to be detached from his own soul. It is far more palatable to follow a man who is in control of his inner world than it is to submit to a man who is inauthentic or guarded.

A Man Must Own His Pain.

The great lie is that women are emotional, and men are not. Wow! What a lie! As men, we are actually more emotional, in many cases. We have a greater reason to be emotional; we are responsible for the entire family. God is holding us responsible. The difference between men and women is in how we express our emotions.

Women Explode with Emotion; Men Implode with Emotion.

Women get it out. They cry, they scream, and they may even beg and plead. We, as men, feel all of the same trauma, anxiety, pressure and fear, but we just hold it within. It destroys us from the inside out. We go into our proverbial caves and fall apart.

A Man Has to Train Himself to Own and Appropriately Express His Feelings When Necessary.

I believe that the first thing a man must do is to decipher where his pain originated and what perpetuates it. Toxic emotion is the consequence of pain. If we are too macho to acknowledge that we hurt, it will be impossible to locate the source. It's like a person who is bent over in pain and is constantly telling the doctor, "Nothing's wrong. I feel fine." It's clear, from the outburst of grunts and groans, that you're not fine, but the doctor can do little for you if you won't acknowledge your condition.

While we as men say, "I'm fine," our emotional tension is dictating that something is happening beneath the surface. Our children and wives see it, even though we think we do a good job of covering it up.

Most of your emotional dysfunction stems from one of two areas: your toxic history or your present perception of possibilities. In other words, the way a man was raised, and how he processes it, will impact his emotional stability. Also, the way a man views his life and his opportunities will drive him emotionally.

> When I See a Man Who Is Emotionally Toxic,
> I Immediately Begin to Analyze His History and
> What Might Be His Present Perception of His Life.

There is tremendous wisdom captured in Proverbs 13:12, where it says: *Hope deferred maketh the heart sick: but when the desire cometh, it is a tree of life.*

When a man has been disappointed in life, it darkens his heart. It reflects in his optimism versus pessimism. When we are in challenging moments, self-understanding and self-analysis are mandatory for self-control. There are a few questions that we must ask and answer for ourselves.

1. WHAT IS YOUR HISTORICAL CONTEXT?

Every man must take into account his historical context. Where you come from, what you've been through and where you presently are as a man carries weight in how you process circumstances and express emotion.

> A Man Would Do Himself a Great Justice If He Would
> Objectively Scrutinize His Own History. He May Connect
> the Dots to His Flaws and Emotional Insecurities.

For instance, when a man has dealt with an absent father as a child, it creates a very real impression of abandonment on his psyche. If you never get delivered from the feelings of abandonment, you may be emotionally triggered every time something remotely resembles rejection. The slightest disagreement may send you into full-blown rejection mode. This can happen in friendships, in love affairs, with children and even in the workplace environment.

Emotion doesn't just float from the sky. It comes from within, and much of it emanates from a toxic history. When I look at my emotional frequency, I can correlate it to my historical context. In other words, I understand why certain things affect me as they do. Because I have this self-perspective, I am simultaneously empowered to harness my emotions before they get out of control.

Here's how this works in my life: I was a teenaged unwed father, and I was the son of the pastor of a Baptist church. This combination of factors brought about a public outcry against my behavior. As a young kid, I did not view the public disdain as being against my behavior; I processed it as hatred for me, personally. This created very strong feelings within me that impacted me emotionally. These emotions went from anger to self-pity. This was a major part of my historical context.

Of course, I grew beyond that moment and the pain it produced. I am in a healthy and more mature place today. However, I still recognize how that history can creep into my present-day assessment of matters and generate emotions that are sometimes unfounded. Sometimes I feel my emotions beginning to rise, in certain situations, and suddenly I remember where these emotions stem from. I take authority over my mind and I judge the matter wisely and soberly, rather than reacting to pain from my childhood.

How Many Men Today Are Having an Emotional Reaction to Childhood Trauma?

The Word of God says, in Hebrews 12:15: *Looking diligently lest any man fail of the grace of God; lest any root of bitterness springing up trouble you, and thereby many be defiled.*

A root of bitterness is simply a historical offense. It is something that happened in the past and is still impacting you emotionally. It springs up into your present life and creates emotional reactions that compromise your judgment and discretion. Many men behave in an emotionally reckless fashion because of something they have not processed from their past.

2. WHAT IS YOUR HONEST PERSPECTIVE ON YOUR LIFE AND ITS POSSIBILITIES?

Have you noticed how tense you become when you discern that your options are few and your challenges are many? When the realization of your dreams is uncertain, it takes its toll, and it may reflect in your emotions. You may find yourself saying things that may require an apology. It's a reaction.

When a Man Feels Cornered, It Creates a Ferocious Frustration.

Sometimes your emotional imbalance is due to a poor perspective on how you view your future. If you do not feel as though you have the opportunities to advance, it will reflect in your attitude. If you feel as though you've been unfairly discriminated against, it will definitely bring your spirit low. A man's positive view of his future is mandatory to emotional health.

Proverbs 29:18 is best known to read like this: *Where there is no vision the people perish.* The same text in the Message Bible version reads: *If people can't see what God is doing, they stumble all over themselves; But when they attend to what He reveals they are most blessed.*

A man must have a firm perspective on his preferred future to navigate the times of pressure and instability. When a man can't see beyond the current predicament, his emotions are inundated with toxic negativity.

Even Jesus demonstrated this need to see beyond the moment into a brighter future. When he was in the Garden of Gethsemane, the reality of the torture that waited ahead got to him. He was contemplating finding another way out, until he thought about where his suffering would bring him.

It is recorded, in Hebrews 12:2: *Looking unto Jesus the author and finisher of our faith; who for the joy that was set before him endured the cross, despising the shame, and is set down at the right hand of the throne of God.*

Jesus, as a man, was able to push through the pressure of temptation and fear, into the promise. He could do this because he knew what was to come. As men, vision is vital to us.

When a Man Doesn't See a Positive Future, He Feels Like a Failure.

This is why the relationship and fellowship with God is so important. God helps a man to see what is beyond the moment. Faith is a key component to a man's emotional health. Faith allows a man to maintain hope in spite of the optics.

It was Abraham's faith that stabilized him in a hopeless situation. Abraham was about one hundred years of age and his wife was too old to conceive. He had hopes of a son and was able to stay steady, because of his faith.

The record is found in Romans 4:19–21, which says: *And being not weak in faith, he considered not his own body now dead, when he was about an hundred years old, neither yet the deadness of Sara's womb: He staggered not at the promise of God through unbelief; but was strong in faith, giving glory to God; And being fully persuaded that, what he had promised, he was able also to perform.*

His faith kept him steady and consistent emotionally. Every man needs a strong faith.

Faith in God Also Produces a Faith in Oneself.

3. HOW DO YOU CONTROL YOUR IMPULSES?

As men we must control our emotional impulses. When we get emotional, we hold the pain within while we exhibit bad behavior. While we are saying, "I'm good," we are kicking the dog. For instance, we may have insecurities about our job's future. We will keep those fears and concerns locked up within our hearts. We won't say to anybody, "I'm afraid." What happens instead is that we snap at people who don't deserve it, or we engage in activities to help us to forget about our real issue. This turns into drinking, adultery or even drugs. It often grows into the destruction of good relationships for no good reason. It all comes down to emotional impulses that were self-sabotaging.

When we don't have a pragmatic program of processing our emotions and controlling our impulses, we become self-destructive and toxic to everybody in close proximity.

A PRACTICAL PROGRAM FOR PERSONAL EMOTIONAL BALANCE

I have discovered that I must have strategies in place to avoid random reactions. The following is my personal program for overcoming emotionally challenging moments or seasons.

> Kings Are Not Unhinged, Nor Are They Ridged.
> Kings Are Always Steady.

A. TALK YOUR FEELINGS OUT

There's nothing more therapeutic than talking. When a man has a safe and trusted space where he may be completely transparent and vulnerable, without getting judged, it allows him to decompress before destruction.

> Wisdom Is Often the Consequence of
> Transparent Conversation.

He's going to want to strangle me for mentioning this, but I must. I won't mention his name. He knows who he is. A friend of mine, who is an author, called me one day in utter frustration. I asked why. He proceeded to explain to me that he was nearly finished a book he had been working on for many months, when his computer screen went black. He could not see any way to retrieve his data. He had not backed anything up to an external drive. He had not sent anything to the cloud. He had his blood, sweat and tears invested in a computer that was now on the blink.

He told me of how he was getting ready to throw it into the trash. He talked about being so frustrated that he had a mind to kick it like a soccer ball. I exclaimed, "No!" I told him that, just because the screen was dead, it didn't mean that his data was lost. The screen was not the computer. I instructed him to bring it to an electronics store and let them look at it. One hour later, he called me, completely relieved. He had his data back. What if he had not talked about it and had just followed his first decision? He would have had to rewrite an entire book, unnecessarily.

How many situations were redeemable, but you trashed them because of uninformed impulses?

The Bible says, in Proverbs 11:14: *Where no counsel is, the people fall: but in the multitude of counsellors there is safety.*

B. CONSIDER THE LONG-TERM CONSEQUENCES

A wise man will learn to pause and ask himself a very serious question: If I do what I feel right now, how long and how much am I going to have to pay for it? Every emotional action has a reaction; sometimes the reaction to the action will last for a lifetime.

How many men are sitting in prison over one emotional moment? They never paused to consider the price.

I remember, as a young man, I was in a public place and I got very angry with a particular person. I was shouting and maybe even using profanity, I was so upset. My mother was close to me and she said, very calmly, "Bob, be quiet." I continued. She then said, "Bob, shut up!" and I continued. Moments later it felt like lightning had struck the right side of my face. My mom had slapped me to bring me down out of the emotional rampage I was on. Once I was quiet, she began to explain to me that a wrong statement in front of such a crowd could cost me the rest of my life.

I was upset with my mom then; but now, as a man, I can understand the lesson she taught me. There are some impulses we have that may serve to cripple our future. We all need to pause and ask: What will be the long-term impact of this momentary impulse?

C. MAKE CERTAIN YOUR IMPULSES AGREE WITH YOUR CORE

As a man, you must always strive to be in sync with your core. Your values and principles may often be compromised by an emotional moment that hasn't been thought through. The man who believes in marriage and fidelity could very easily have an impulse that brings him down a road filled with contradictions, shame and compromise.

> Every Man Must Think About What He's Thinking About and See If It Aligns with Who He Is and What He Believes.

Our emotions may very easily disrupt our integrity if we do not challenge and compare them against our character.

Have you ever had the feeling that you wanted to do something, and when you gave it your full attention, you realized that it disagreed with who you are? Never allow a random emotion to dictate your behavior. *You* are to dictate your emotions; not the other way around.

The Word of God challenges us in Luke 21:19, where it states: *In your patience possess ye your souls*. The term "soul" speaks of the mind, will and emotion. Always be in possession of your soul.

When a king is in control of his emotions, he leaves no room for anyone to usurp his power. He becomes the best leader he may be and he lives a life of integrity, maturity and consistency. You, my brother, are a king. Walk like it.

Conclusion

For a long time, I have desired to create a document that would capture some of my thoughts and feelings about manhood. My hope is that this book will serve as a proxy and communicate my heart and spirit to every man who reads it.

There are principles about manhood that are best communicated from king to king. I believe that this medium of writing and reading is potent and can transform a man's world. The chapters in this book are some of the principles I live by on a daily basis. These are the things that were modeled and taught to me by my father.

There is no greater honor than to be a man who is respected as a man, because he "walks his talk." When you are done with this book, remember that manhood is action. Your entire community is waiting on you to be what is needed. This is the hour when the kings must return to the kingdom. We have enough clowns; let the kings rise.

My prayer for you is that the Almighty will purge your heart from every sense of guilt and shame, relative to your past. This is about moving forward. All of the mistakes and failures of your life will produce wisdom for your rise and reign. It's not where you've been or who you were that's important; it's who you are and where you're going.